WRITE BETTER,
SPEAK BETTER ENGLISH

The ability to speak and write
correct English can be one of the most
important tools in your future.
This lucid, authoritative guide to
proper usage contains helpful hints
on every aspect of English grammar,
spelling and punctuation, with a
special supplement on how to write
reports, research papers, and letters.

A CONCISE HANDBOOK OF BETTER ENGLISH

A CONCISE HANDBOOK
OF BETTER ENGLISH

·

BY ROGER B. GOODMAN

CHAIRMAN, DEPARTMENT OF ENGLISH,
STUYVESANT HIGH SCHOOL,
NEW YORK CITY

A CONCISE HANDBOOK OF BETTER ENGLISH
Bantam Reference Library edition published November 1962
Bantam Desk edition published March 1966

Library of Congress Catalog Card Number: 62-20939

Published simultaneously in the United States and Canada

Bantam Books are published by Bantam Books, Inc., a subsidiary
of Grosset & Dunlap, Inc. Its trade-mark, consisting of the words
"Bantam Books" ana the portrayal of a bantam, is registered in the
United States Patent Office and in other countries. Marca Registrada.
Bantam Books, Inc., 271 Madison Avenue, New York, N. Y. 10016.

PRINTED IN THE UNITED STATES OF AMERICA

CONTENTS

I am indebted to the following people who read the manuscript and made valuable suggestions: my father, Henry Goodman, formerly of the New York City High School system and Hunter College; Enid S. Russell; and David Sohn, Department of Study Skills, Yale University.

I. THE PARTS OF SPEECH

A. Noun, Pronoun, Verb

- *Nuts!*
- *We shall fight on the beaches, we shall fight on the landing grounds, we shall fight in the fields and in the streets, we shall fight in the hills; we shall never surrender.*

- *G'night, honey. See you tomorrow.*
- *Good night, good night! parting is such sweet sorrow, That I shall say good night till it be morrow.*

- *O.K.! O.K.! There's nothing to be scared of!*
- *The only thing we have to fear is fear itself.*

By now, I'm sure, the point is clear. No one who reads can fail to understand the preceding phrases. And, surely, we can recall or reconstruct the occasions of their utterance: General Anthony McAuliffe at Bastogne, Winston Churchill in Parliament; any one young lover to another, Juliet to Romeo; any leader reassuring his followers, President Franklin D. Roosevelt reassuring all Americans.

All communication is language. Any grunt, groan or whimper can convey meaning and thus become language—of a sort. Simple words, bluntly put can carry meaning and feeling as well. Yet what distinguishes each second sentence in the groups above is not clarity of meaning or even correctness of address; it is something which we call eloquence—the injection of beauty and expression into language, which adds pleasure to understanding and charm to use.

This book cannot promise that every person can become the verbal magician Churchill is. But it does stoutly maintain that everyone **can learn to express himself directly,**

accurately and correctly; and with these three graces exercising their powers—directness, accuracy and correctness—expression can frequently be given simple beauty.

To achieve the absolute mastery that our mission calls for, we shall begin at the traditional beginning, making no assumptions, and work through the entire realm of rule and theory, principle and exception, the do's and don'ts of English grammar.

The foundation stone of language is the word. And because the word appears in many guises, it is necessary to identify it however it may be used. In this process of identification, we speak of PRINCIPAL PARTS OF SPEECH. These are no less essential and no more difficult to distinguish than dashboard from tail gate, strike from ball and driver from putter.

The NOUN is one of the most important elements of our language. To verify this, let us repeat that sentence without the nouns:

The —— is one of the most important —— of our ——.

What is now missing in the sentence prevents us from deriving any meaning from this cluster of words.

By definition, **the noun is a word used to indicate a person, place or thing.** Thus, within the definition itself we have the following nouns:

1. _noun_
2. _word_
3. _person_
4. _place_
5. _thing_

To be more particular, a noun names

a person or persons:
boy, man, angel, women, children

a place or places:
city, seashore, countries

a thing or things:
desk, cars, freedom,* beauty,* pencils

NOTE: These nouns are general in nature, indicating a universal type rather than any **one particular item.** The words marked with an asterisk indicate intangible, abstract things which are no less **real** because they are **ideas** rather than objects with size, shape and dimension.

Sometimes nouns are difficult to recognize because they parade under false colors. Consider, for example, *hunting*. As the word appears here it may be called a form of the verb *to hunt*. How do we know, then, that it is not a verb? First, no *-ing* form of any verb, **when used alone,** functions as a verb; secondly, the word *hunting* is the **name of an activity** or of a concept, like *swimming, running, breathing*. The test, therefore, is valid: if the word names an idea or a concept, it is a noun.

Because these nouns **refer to broad, all-inclusive classes of things,** they are called COMMON NOUNS.

Other nouns, however, have a sharply restricted use and a special meaning. These are called PROPER NOUNS. They refer only to **specific** persons, places or things, and are distinguished by being spelled with initial capital letters. Thus:

COMMON NOUN	PROPER NOUN
ship	*Queen Elizabeth*
president	*President Kennedy*
house	*White House*

Each of us lives with the most familiar of proper nouns, his own name: *Roger B. Goodman, John W. Smith* and the renowned *John Doe*.

John told John's friend that John was going to drive John's car to John's father's house.

What is wrong with the foregoing sentence? Obviously an overworking of the name *John*. With the **pronoun, a word used in place of, or to stand for, a noun,** the offensive sentence above could be rewritten as follows:

John told **his** *friend that* **he** *was going to drive* **his** *car to* **his** *father's house.*

Though an improvement over the first version, this sentence now illustrates some of the pitfalls of using pronouns. Is *his* car John's car, or that of the friend? We're fairly certain that it means John's car, but, as the Army phrases it, "If it **can** be misunderstood, it **will** be misunderstood." This difficulty is called **indefiniteness or uncertainty of antecedent.** It arises when we're not sure what the pronoun refers to. The error and its correction will be dealt with later. First, let us definitely establish the types and functions of pronouns.

In the preceding paragraph, you will notice the frequent use of the word *it*. This common pronoun is a favorite device for avoiding repetition of nouns. Can you think of the nouns which would have been used, had *it* not been there?

If we think of the pronoun as a "stand-in" for a noun, in the sense that an actor can be a "stand-in" for a star, we shall be able to see certain important facts.

1. There must be **agreement** between the noun and the pronoun that takes its place **in gender:** (Rosalind Russell, for example, could hardly "stand in" for John Wayne!)

NOUN	PRONOUN
man (male star)	*he-his-him* (male stand-in)
woman (female star)	*she-hers-her* (female stand-in)
desk (any prop)	*it-its-it* (neuter stand-in)

NOTE: The neuter gender attributed to **things** and, frequently, to animals is indicated by the neuter pronoun *it*.

2. There must be **agreement in number:**

NOUN	PRONOUN
boy (singular)	*he-his-him* (singular)
boys (plural)	*they-their(s)-them* (plural)
girls (plural)	*they-their(s)-them* (plural)
desks (plural)	*they-their(s)-them* (plural)

NOTE: In the plural there is no distinction among male, female and neuter forms of the pronoun.

3. There must be **agreement in case:**

NOUN	PRONOUN
1. The **man** works.	**He** works.
2. The car struck the **man.**	The car struck **him.**
3. It is the **man's** hat.	It is **his** hat.

In sentence 1 the noun *man* is in the NOMINATIVE CASE. This means that *man* is **the performer of the action.**

In sentence 2 the noun *man* is in the OBJECTIVE CASE; the *man* **receives the action of the verb.**

In sentence 3 *man's* is in the POSSESSIVE CASE, **showing ownership.**

SINGULAR NOUN	PRONOUN: NOMINATIVE CASE	PRONOUN: OBJECTIVE CASE	PRONOUN: POSSESSIVE CASE
man (masculine)	*he*	*him*	*his*
lady (feminine)	*she*	*her*	*her(s)*
chair (neuter)	*it*	*it*	*its*
PLURAL NOUN:			
kings (masculine)	*they*	*them*	*their(s)*
girls (feminine)	*they*	*them*	*their(s)*
cars (neuter)	*they*	*them*	*their(s)*

The first person pronoun *I* and the second person pronoun *you* do not, in a sense, really stand in for nouns.

SINGULAR:	*I*	*me*	*mine (my)*
	you	*you*	*your(s)*
PLURAL:	*we*	*us*	*our(s)*
	you	*you*	*your(s)*

To determine the correct pronoun, fall back upon the assistance of your ears. Certain expressions just **sound right.** For example, suppose you were asked to substitute the correct pronoun in the sentence:

My **mother** *cooks well.*

Try saying it out loud. Would you say, "Her cooks well?" Hardly. Obviously what we are looking for is "She cooks well."

Again, what pronoun would you substitute for the following?

Ship the cars to New York.

Ship *they* to New York? No. Our ears quickly tell us it's "Ship *them* to New York." And we may use this device to help with our knowledge of nominative and objective cases.

NOTE: A detailed study of the cases will be found in the section dealing with grammatical functions.

There are certain rules of preferred usage that affect the choice of certain pronouns. Notice the word *that* in the preceding sentence. It is a pronoun. In this special use, it is called a RELATIVE PRONOUN: it introduces a restrictive or limiting element. The relative pronoun *which* introduces a non-restrictive element (one that could be omitted without changing the meaning of the main clause). Thus, "Certain rules, *which* are not difficult to learn, affect the choice. . ." Their preferred usage is in reference to places and things.

Under similar circumstances, if we refer to people we use the pronouns *who* and *whom:* "The man (that, who) said it" or "The man to (which, whom) I spoke." Here *who* and *whom* are correct.

To generalize: *that* and *which* refer to things; *who* and *whom* refer to persons.

A small group of specialized pronouns are characterized by their violation of one of the standard rules of spelling. These words are the POSSESSIVE PRONOUNS. They all end with the letter *s*, and none of them uses the apostrophe, the normal symbol of possession. These possessive pronouns are:

> *his*
> *hers*
> *yours*
> *ours*
> *theirs*
> *its*

Instead of accompanying any particular word, six of these terms will stand alone. Thus:

> *It is* **their** *house.*

but

> *The house is* **theirs.**

The exception is *its,* which is used to show simple possession on the part of any single, nonhuman object:

> *The snow has lost* **its** *charm.*

We have stated that the noun, with its stand-in, the pronoun, is one of the two principal parts of speech. **The other member of the powerful duo is the verb.** Let us repeat the first sentence of this paragraph, this time without the verbs:

> *We* —— *that the noun, with its stand-in, the pronoun,* —— *one of the two principal parts of speech.*

We have a fine, impressive hulk, but no motive power. There is no life or motion. If the noun provides the body, the verb provides the heart.

What, specifically, do we mean by VERB? The verb is the word which **designates action** or indicates a **state of being.** This is a way of saying that everything either **does** or **is** something.

VERB OF ACTION: Action can be physical or mental. If running, jumping, flying and hitting represent action, so do thinking, pondering, musing and dreaming. An action of any sort is indicated by a verb.

STATE-OF-BEING VERB: A more technical name for this is *copulative* or linking verb. Such a verb reveals no action. It states that something simply exists. The English verb which expresses the concept of existence is, of course, *to be.* Why is this verb called a "copulative," or "coupling" verb?

> *It* **is** *a verb.*

Notice, in this last sentence, that while no action is performed, a relationship is established between *it* and *verb.* The nature of the relationship, the link, is provided by the verb *is.*

While it is easy to recognize this particular nonaction verb, there are others which are not so obvious.

> *The rose* smells *sweet.*
> *The car* appears *undamaged.*
> *You* look *well.*

Each of these verbs—*smells, appears, look*—is basically a word denoting action. But in the three sentences above, no action is involved: the rose is not **doing the smelling,** nor is the car **performing the act of appearing** nor are you **doing any looking.** In each case the verb is a link, a coupling between *rose* and *sweet, car* and *undamaged, you* and *well.* Once again, then, we have copulative verbs, state-of-being verbs, though they are not part of the verb *to be.* A sure test of the copulative nature of any verb is to substitute some form of the verb *to be* for it. If the sentence makes sense without changing its meaning, the verb is a state-of-being verb. Thus:

The rose smells *sweet. The rose* is *sweet.*

The car appears *undamaged. The car* is *undamaged.*

You look *well. You* are *well.*

Another important point must be observed in dealing with the verb. The *-ing* form of the verb, called the PRESENT PARTICIPLE, cannot stand by itself as a verb. One cannot say:

Being *a man*

or

Seeing *the sun rise*

with any sense of completeness. In these cases the verb, called a participle, is used to introduce a group of words called a PARTICIPIAL PHRASE.

Being a man, *he had greater strength.*

or

Seeing the sun rise, *he made breakfast.*

The participle is also used as a single modifier.

The **flying** *horse was called Pegasus.*

or

The **whirling** *plate was smashed.*

Here the participle is used to **modify** a noun, thus being used as an adjective, a term we will study more closely in the next section.

Before we leave the noun, pronoun and verb, however, we should turn our attention briefly to how these are combined. When we have noun and verb, we have the root ingredients for the most significant constructed element in our language, the SENTENCE. The following equation is vital to our tongue:

NOUN (PRONOUN) + VERB + MODIFIERS = SENTENCE

The sentence is the core of communication. In the equation the noun assumes a new title; it is called a SUBJECT. To discuss the complex nature of our grammar, we are going to employ an ancient, honorable device which enables some aspects of English to become almost scientifically precise. This device is the **diagram.** Every sentence, no matter how long and complicated, can be fitted into a diagram so that, like an X-ray plate, it can be thoroughly analyzed.

In proper diagrams a few simple rules hold:

1. **All nouns, pronouns and verbs are placed on horizontal lines.**
2. **All modifiers and connectives are on diagonal or vertical lines.**

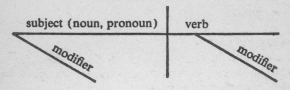

In its simplest form, a simple sentence, diagramed, would appear this way:

The ship sailed.

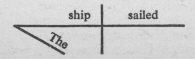

Keep the image and concept in mind. We will explore further, and make the device prove its worth.

EXERCISE 1. Name Your Nouns

A. Choose a short paragraph from the nearest paper, magazine or book. Make a list of all common nouns and then one of proper nouns.

B. Underline **all the nouns** in the following paragraph. (Answers on p. 131.)

Every spring sees the resumption of a great American ritual. People who normally love to sleep late set their alarms for five o'clock in the morning, shake the sleep from their bleary eyes, and stagger out to their cars. After a drive that might last for an hour, they find themselves with hundreds of other early risers, signing a roster, reserving a spot on the links for hours later, and then finding their way back home to sleep until game time.

EXERCISE 2. The Pronoun

A. Rewrite the following sentences making intelligent use of pronouns. (Answers on p. 131.)

1. Frank told Frank's father, Tom, that Tom ought to play golf.
2. Tom, Frank's father, explained to Tom's son that Frank's father could not play golf.
3. Tom's wife told Tom's wife's husband that Tom and Tom's son should both play golf so that Tom's wife could have some peace on Sundays.

B. Choose the correct pronoun in each case. (Answers on p. 131.)

1. They offered Mary and (I, me) a lift.
2. (Me and Mary, Mary and me, Mary and I) refused.
3. Then (him, he) and Frank drove home.
4. Soon I noticed that (Frank and him, Frank and he) were annoyed.

5. So (<u>Mary and I,</u> me and Mary, Mary and me) joined (<u>Frank and him,</u> he and Frank) for a little drive.

EXERCISE 3. The Verb

Make a list of all the verbs in the following paragraph. Put an *s* beside all the "state-of-being" verbs. (Answers on p. 131.)

It will be a matter of great debate as to who should have the title of King of Swat. The old-timers tend to be loyal to George Herman Ruth. The Babe's name still stirs the blood. There is still the picture in men's minds of the Babe at bat, pointing to the spot where he would hit his next homer. But the youngsters count numbers. They point out that sixty-one is more than sixty—and that settles that.

B. Adjective, Adverb

Life can be lived in gray, rocky caves, and probably was by generations of humans over thousands of years. Then someone, tired of staring at bare walls, drew or gouged some figures of men and animals and made the walls somewhat pleasanter to look at. (This is not to deny whatever ritual purposes might have been served.) Much later, in days of pottery, unadorned jugs and plates were replaced by utensils which bore the touch of the decorator as well as that of the toolmaker. Function and beauty were combined.

If the modifying touch of beauty is found in many aspects of men's external lives, how could it be excluded from language, man's most intimate, potent and widely used tool? The distance from "Me, Tarzan—You, Jane!" to:

> *What's in a name? That which we call a rose*
> *By any other name would smell as sweet:*
> *So Romeo would, were he not Romeo called,*

> *Retain that dear perfection which he owes*
> *Without the title.*

is the span that separates barbarism from civilization, and mere existence from cultivated life. Language now communicates, but with degrees of precision, with the play of individuality and with the use of imagination. Language can, more than any other human attribute, declare the individual, the unique "I," which is different from all others, though sharing basic similarities.

How is the shading accomplished? Where does the secret lie? Basically it is in the **modifiers:** the ADJECTIVE and the ADVERB.

The adjective is an adjunct or modifier of a noun or pronoun. In other words an adjective tells something specific about the noun or pronoun it accompanies. In the broadest sense it describes the word it modifies. Thus:

> *He saw a girl.*

Of moderate interest, this. But watch:

> *He saw a* **beautiful** *girl.*

Something happens. The adjective *beautiful* tells us something about the girl. But tastes vary. Let us be more specific:

> *He saw a* **tall, beautiful** *girl.*

The image becomes clearer. If we happen to dislike tall girls, this quality does not especially attract us. But we begin to see a picture.

> *He saw a* **tall, beautiful, redheaded** *girl.*

This gives her hair color, a general description of her beauty. Let us establish a rule: the adjective modifies a noun or pronoun and describes it in terms of:

> size
> shape
> color
> texture
> quality

The adjective performs an additional function: it **limits** (or indicates the number of) the noun (pronoun) it accompanies:

He saw **three tall, beautiful, redheaded** *girls*.

Let us return for a moment to the diagram we introduced in the previous section. You will recall the pattern:

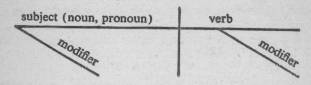

Here is our sentence:

The beautiful redheaded girl departed.

What kind of girl? "Beautiful."
Any other description? "Redheaded."

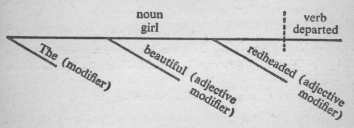

Each separate adjective directly modifies the noun *girl*, a "beautiful girl," a "redheaded girl." A large number of adjectives may modify any one noun or pronoun.

In our language the adjective usually appears immediately before the noun it modifies. This principle varies occasionally. In the interests of eloquence and variety of expression a writer may shift adjectives about. For example:

The **angry** *man revealed a* **furious, red** *face.*
Angry, *the man revealed a face* **red** *with fury.*

We have learned that the noun and pronoun may be given terms to enhance their meanings. The verb also shares this privilege. For not only can language describe variously what one is, it can also indicate variations in what one does. **The word which modifies the verb is called an adverb.** The adverb will tell us:

1. how
2. when
3. where
4. to what degree

Thus:

> *She runs*

is a colorless enough statement. But let us add shading:

> *She runs* (how?) **gracefully.**
> *She runs* (when?) **daily.**
> *She runs* (where?) **here.**

In other words, the adverb gives specific information about an action or state of being.

In our diagram we would see this:

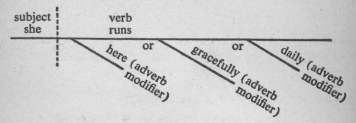

But the adverb is the most versatile and fickle of words. It is a term of divided loyalties. It serves as an adjunct not only to the verb but also to the adjective, even to another adverb. Let us examine this mystery by returning to our redheaded beauty.

> *He saw a tall, beautiful, redheaded girl.*

Suppose we add another element:

> *He* **immediately** *saw a tall, beautiful, redheaded girl.*

When did he "saw"? Immediately!

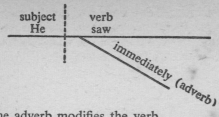

Here the adverb modifies the verb.
Again:

He saw an extremely tall, beautiful, redheaded girl.

What does *extremely* tell us something about? How tall was she? Not *very* tall, not *fairly* tall, but *extremely* tall.

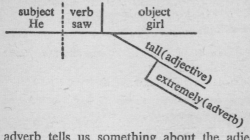

The adverb tells us something about the adjective, a refinement of the refinement.

The adverb can also modify another adverb. Here we may be stretching a point in reasonable usage. The phrasing does, however, occur occasionally.

> *He **very frequently** saw an extremely tall,*
> *beautiful, redheaded girl.*

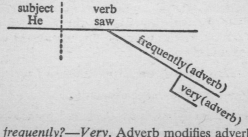

How *frequently?*—*Very*. Adverb modifies adverb!

Another attribute is shared by adjective and adverb; they must be varied to indicate changing degrees. The degrees are referred to as POSITIVE, COMPARATIVE and SUPERLATIVE. Let us take the adjectives first. Some are irregular in the way they are compared.

POSITIVE	COMPARATIVE	SUPERLATIVE
good	*better*	*best*
much	*more*	*most*
bad	*worse*	*worst*
little	*less*	*least*

When they are regular, they add *-er* and *-est* to the root, or positive form. This is particularly true when the word is short, a monosyllable, or if it ends in *-ly*. For example:

POSITIVE	COMPARATIVE	SUPERLATIVE
wise	*wis*er	*wis*est
large	*larg*er	*larg*est
lovely	*loveli*er	*loveli*est

Suppose, however, we encounter *peculiar*. "He had a *peculiar* look on his face." Our ears rebel at "But his friend had a peculiarer look." So we resort to the helpful words *more* and *most,* and *less* and *least.*

POSITIVE	COMPARATIVE	SUPERLATIVE
peculiar	*less/more peculiar*	*least/most peculiar*
ridiculous	*less/more ridiculous*	*least/most ridiculous*
influential	*less/more influential*	*least/most influential*

In similar fashion adverbs may be compared.

He shouted **harshly.**
She answered (harshlier?—certainly not!) **more harshly.**
And the trump play is *most* **harshly.**

Here, then, is the adverbial pattern:

POSITIVE	COMPARATIVE	SUPERLATIVE
harshly	*less/more harshly*	*least/most harshly*
pleasantly	*less/more pleasantly*	*least/most pleasantly*
quaintly	*less/more quaintly*	*least/most quaintly*

Bear in mind that an ear attuned to correct speech patterns can sometimes prove to be a valuable aid in determining proper usage. It's like writing out words to have a look at them in order to see if they are spelled correctly. It doesn't always work, but it's always worth trying.

EXERCISE 4. Words for Flavor

A. List separately all the adjectives and all the adverbs you find in a magazine paragraph. NOTE: many adverbs are formed by adding "ly" to an adjective: loud–loud*ly*; willing–willing*ly*.

B. Here are some rather drab sentences. Improve them with meaningful, colorful adjectives instead of those italicized. (See p. 131 for example.)

1. The Joneses bought a *nice* new home.
2. They thought it was in a *lovely* neighborhood.
3. They were thrilled by the *nice* view of the water.
4. Then they noticed certain *bad* features of the house.
5. The *lovely* cellar kept the water in instead of out.

EXERCISE 5.

Now try your hand at diagraming. At this point let us concentrate on adjectives and adverbs. (Answers on p. 132.)

1. Big, bad John died bravely.
2. The huge, gnarled, oak timbers cracked.
3. Frightened, shouting miners fled swiftly.
4. John stood stiffly.
5. The crumbling coal roared loudly, mercilessly down.

C. Conjunction, Preposition

"We must all hang together," said Ben Franklin, "or assuredly we shall all hang separately."

This is equally true of sentences except for a slight twist. For though sentences do stand alone, they most assuredly are hung together. The words which have the task of hanging sentences or ideas together are called CONJUNCTIONS and PREPOSITIONS. In making ideas clear, or at least understood, the conjunction and preposition are less important than the noun and verb, but they do smooth the rough edges. They provide the easy transition, the subtle distinction, the drastic contrast which make language effective.

As a **connective,** the conjunction serves a double purpose. It may link two words or phrases of **equal** value, or it may tie a **subordinate** or **dependent theme** to one which is superior or independent. **A conjunction which relates two items of equal importance is called a** CO-ORDINATING CONJUNCTION. The word *and* is the prime conjunction. The elements thus joined are **compound** constructions: **compound subject, compound verb, compound modifier, compound sentence.** Let us examine some evidence.

Compound Subject

> *Chevalier* **and** *Crosby are world-famous singers.*
>
> Note that each name is of equal importance. The order could be reversed and no harm to the meaning would be done. The terms are **coordinate,** of equal weight.

Compound Object

> *The gown was threaded with silver* **and** *gold.*
>
> Again we have two equal terms linked by *and.* We could reverse the order to "gold **and** silver," and change only the visual concept, not the grammatical structure.

Compound Sentence

> *She stayed,* **but** *I left.*
>
> Here, though a somewhat finer distinction is drawn, the coordinate-equal concept remains. No cause and effect relationship is established, nor any other dependency. This construction is called a COMPOUND SENTENCE: that is, a sentence consisting of two equal, independent parts linked by a coordinating conjunction.

Some conjunctions called CORRELATIVES are distinguished by the fact that they are used in pairs:

> **Either** *you tell her,* **or** *I shall.*
> **Neither** *you* **nor** *your friend will fail!*

In this case two words are sent to do the work of one, but the coordinate linking process remains the same.

Let us resort, once again, to the diagram to demonstrate the theoretical points we have made. How shall we show the **coordinate** (or equal) relationship of several nouns?

John, Thomas, **and** *Ebenezer sleep.*

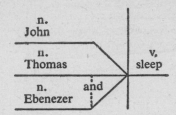

Suppose now that one person performs several actions.

Rigoletto sang, raged, roared **and** *fumed!*

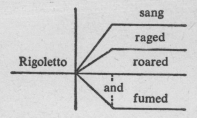

For the sake of grammatical clarity let us make a rather foolish combination.

Ebenezer slept **and** *Rigoletto fumed!*

	Ebenezer	slept
and	Rigoletto	fumed

The key point to remember is that coordinates are equal in importance; no one element depends upon the other.

Another construction is possible, however. It occurs when one grammatical unit cannot stand alone and is subordinate to, or dependent upon another element. Here a SUBORDINATING CONJUNCTION is used. We shall illustrate without elaborating. (A more detailed study will be made later.)

When *the whistle blew, the game commenced.*

Break the sentence into two parts: **"When** the whistle blew" obviously cannot stand by itself. Visualize a freight car, loaded, ready to move, with its coupling device outstretched. "The game commenced" is clearly independent; it stands alone. Visualize here the locomotive, filled with energy and strength, which needs no assistance to move.

Here, then, are our two types of units. The independent clause is a sentence in itself. The dependent or subordinate clause is here introduced by a **subordinating conjunction,** *when.*

For the moment let this illustration suffice. When we discuss clauses and different types of sentences, we will probe much deeper.

The preposition is a small word with power and importance far beyond its apparent significance. This gnat of a word aroused the fury of Sir Winston Churchill when he cried, "That is a bit of nonsense up with which I will not put!" He was mocking the ancient, honorable grammarian's decree, "Never end a sentence with a preposition." Churchill probably helped weaken the argument somewhat. In any event, the usage is now generally acceptable, except in very formal writing and speech.

Let us look at the preposition and see just how influential it is in our language. We shall repeat the opening sentence without the preposition:

Let us look —— the preposition and see
just how influential it is —— our language.

Note how the preposition serves to link words and establish a relationship between them. The preposition will indicate whether we look *"for* the word," *"over* the word" *"beyond* the word," *"into* the word" or *"at* the word." It will also show whether the word is influential *"for* our language," *"within* our language" or *"in* our language."

The preposition, then, is a **linking word which establishes a relationship between two words or groups of words.** Some further characteristics of the preposition are worthy of note. **It is always followed directly, or a word or two later, by a noun or a pronoun.** (Unless, of course, it is used to end a sentence **with!**) Such a construction is called a **prepositional phrase,** about which we will talk more later.

The final member of our group of small but important words is perhaps the least significant, but it is surely the most expressive. The INTERJECTION or **exclamation** is an independent expression of sudden emotion, of shock, fear, dismay, great pleasure. It is usually punctuated with an exclamation point and is easily recognized:

Ah! Distinctly I remember . . .
Ho! Ho! Ho! The hurricane roared!

or simply

Ouch!

EXERCISE 6. A Bit of Review

We have discussed the principal parts of speech: noun, pronoun, verb, adjective, adverb, conjunction, preposition, interjection. Let us wander through the following paragraph and see if we can identify each italicized word. (Answers on p. 133.)

What! Is that all *we* have to do! We *read* page after *page of technical* material, and then we *have* to take tests. Of course, it *is* true that we *can learn this* way. In these *exercises* we can test what we have learned. If we skip the *little* quizzes and *tests,* we will *really* gain only *part* of what is intended. After all, the *best way* to learn how *to use* a new *tool* is to use *it.* And *this* is certainly true *of grammar.*

II. THE SENTENCE (1)

Some eighteenth-century English philosophers compared the universe to a vast watch which the Almighty had hurled into space, jolted into motion and left to operate according to its own natural laws. Discover and understand these laws, declared these thinkers, and all human and natural problems can be dealt with.

In the much more restricted area of grammar we have set the parts of a machine into their proper places. We have now to give motion to our machine; we must give it life.

In the course of our study of correct usage, we will make much of the importance of complete, comprehensible sentences. Fully developed sentences are not at all necessary to communication. We grunt; we jerk out monosyllables; we gesture with our hands, shoulders or eyebrows—and our meaning is clear. Ordinary conversation omits dozens of unexpressed but clearly understood words.

Eat?
Not yet! You?
Not hungry! Smoke?
Thanks. Light?
Got my own. Thanks, anyway.

Does anyone need the full script?

(Did you) *eat?*
(I have) *not yet* (eaten). (Have) *you?*
(I am) *not hungry.* (Would you like a) *smoke?*

Certainly no more is necessary here. Why, then, the great insistence on writing correct sentences and on having generations of students ask and answer in full sentences? Thoughts which are monosyllabically clear can be thoroughly beclouded in a properly constructed sentence. But there is an esthetic element in an orderly, well-constructed presentation of words that is pleasing to listen to or to read. The appeal of correct language can be compared with the pleasure and satisfaction gained by leaving a work bench in neat array or in piling your tricks in bridge at precise right angles. We do get pleasure from doing things correctly!

More than that, language is such a magnificent instrument that its fullest effectiveness is gained with its greatest precision.

Let us, then, turn our attention to the roots from which the towering oaks of eloquent English soar. The first unit— beyond the word—is the sentence.

A sentence is **a group of words containing a subject and a verb, which expresses a complete thought.**

By using some of the information we have already mastered, we can derive this equation:

NOUN (PRONOUN) $+$ VERB $+$ COMPLETED THOUGHT $=$ SENTENCE

One further adjustment needs to be made, however. Instead of merely saying *noun or pronoun* we use the more technical term SUBJECT. The equation then becomes:

SUBJECT $+$ VERB $+$ COMPLETED THOUGHT $=$ SENTENCE

Every function has its terminology, so let us define our terms.

The verb is the word or a group of words **specifying the action performed.**

Where no action is indicated, we have a **copulative** or **linking** or **state-of-being verb.** The major example is the verb *to be* in all its forms.

What, exactly, does this mean?

A man **runs.** Action verb: **runs.**
The car **raced** *along the street.* Action verb: **raced.**
It **is** *a warm day.* State-of-being verb: **is.**
The cat **nipped** *the mouse.* Action verb: **nipped.**

In every sentence **there must be a verb** which will reveal either **action** or **state-of-being.** It is the core of the sentence. A verb can also establish the time of an event or situation through **tenses,** the formation and full meaning of which we will discuss further along.

Our diagraming at this stage will be:

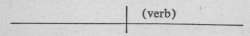

The **subject is a noun or pronoun which performs the action mentioned or which is referred to by the state-of-being verb.** In other words, the subject is the element which **does** or which **is.** We already have the verb. If we now ask **before the verb**—*who or what?*—the answer will give us the subject.

This is an absolutely foolproof way to find the subject of any sentence.

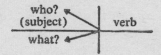

The blonde waltzed.

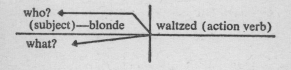

The night was cold.

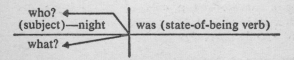

Suppose there is no visible subject.

Stop! or *Wait!*

Are these complete sentences even though they consist of only one word? Yes! Observe!

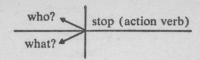

Obviously the person who should stop is the person being told to: *you*. We call this having *"you* (**understood**)" as the subject. In other words, the subject word is not expressed. However, the subject would become painfully apparent if we continued to walk blithely through a military post because we did not recognize the subject of the sentry's shouted *Halt!*

The diagram is completed thus:

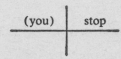

This is most obvious in a command or **imperative** sentence.

Advancing one step further, we note that the subject of a verb is always in the **nominative case**. It is as simple as that!

Just as there **must be a performer** of every action mentioned by the verb in a sentence, so there **may be a receiver** of such action. The performer is called the **subject**; the receiver is called the DIRECT OBJECT. And it, too, will be a noun or pronoun. To put it into a more formal definition: **the object of an action verb is the noun or pronoun which receives the action of that verb.**

He **threw** *the ball.*

The verb *threw* transmits its action to *ball;* hence, *ball* is the **direct object of the verb.**

The recipe for finding the **direct object** of any action verb is to ask *whom* or *what?* **after the verb.** Thus:

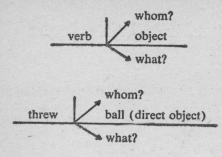

But watch closely!

He threw blindly.

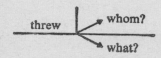

Notice that there is no answer in the sentence to these questions; hence, there is no object.

Remember, then, that an action verb **may have** an object, but it **does not need** one.

To recapitulate: A sentence is a functional unit containing a subject and a verb and expressing a complete thought, with or without an object. In diagram form this is what we see:

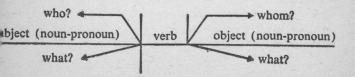

EXERCISE 7.

A. We're getting into deeper water now. In the following sentences pick out the subjects, the verbs and the objects (if there are any objects). (Answers on p. 133-4.)

1. The morning sun rose over the mountains.
2. Did you see the sunrise?
3. The forest threw a shadow on the plain.
4. It was beautiful to see.
5. Look!

B. Here is some more complicated diagraming. (Answers on p. 134.)

1. Maris hit his first home run today.
2. Mantle got his homer too.
3. The season has really started.
4. President Kennedy threw out the first ball.
5. Will the Mets win their pennant immediately?

C. Can you recognize the difference between complete and incomplete sentences? Make the necessary additions. (Example on p. 135.)

1. It came Out of the blue!
2. I never thought I'd ever see such a sight!
3. A flying elephant! It was
4. Not really? Like something out of Disney.
5. Whatever I tell my wife, she'll think my imagination is responsible.

III. PHRASES AND CLAUSES

We have analyzed and stressed the importance of the whole unit in grammar, the complete sentence. Now let us survey the nature and function of the fragmentary groups of words—the phrase or the clause, which, though it be a dependent or subordinate unit, is entitled to full consideration.

There is, first of all, the completely detached cluster of words: "Why not now?" "Certainly not." "Sometimes in the morning." While these phrases cannot stand independently, they will convey meaning when used in context.

Somewhat more organized, though still dependent, is the group of words introduced by a preposition called a PREPOSITIONAL PHRASE. In the vast majority of cases this type of phrase exercises a modifying function and, therefore, takes its name from either of the modifiers, **adjective** or **adverb**. A phrase which describes or limits a noun or pronoun is an ADJECTIVE PHRASE. If it modifies a verb, an adjective or an adverb, it is called an ADVERBIAL PHRASE. In diagram form, these would appear as follows:

The man **in the room** *awoke* **in the morning.**

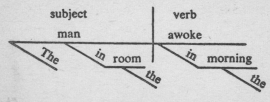

which man?   awoke when?

in the room: adjective phrase modifying *man*
in the morning: adverbial phrase modifying *awoke*

Note how, in diagraming the phrase, the noun is placed on the horizontal line and the preposition and modifiers on the diagonals.

In the phrase, the function of the preposition is to introduce the phrase itself and to establish a relationship between the **word immediately before the preposition** and the **first noun or pronoun following it.** Thus, in the example above, the preposition *in* defines the relationship between the noun *man* and the noun *room.* In the same way the preposition *in* establishes a bridge between the verb *awoke* and the noun *morning.*

Let us proceed to another facet of the same problem. We now have a group of words which contains a subject and a verb **but which does not express a complete thought.** This unit is called a DEPENDENT or SUBORDINATE CLAUSE. Like the phrase, it too functions as a modifier—adjective or adverbial—and is therefore designated an **adjective clause** or **adverbial clause.**

The man **who was in the room** *awoke* **when the sun rose.**

NOTE: Which man? The man *who was in the room:* an adjective clause.

When did he awaken? *when the sun rose:* an adverbial clause.

Follow closely now as we explore the intricacies of the subordinate clause.

. . . who was in the room . . .

This is a subordinate (dependent) clause, an adjective clause modifying the noun *man.* In order to be such a clause it must contain a subject and a verb, but not express a complete thought.

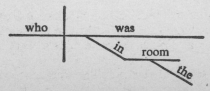

This is how we would diagram the clause.

We are not asking the question, *Who was in the room?* In this case it **would be** an independent clause, indeed an interrogative sentence or question. This clause answers the question, *Which man?* and is, therefore, an adjective clause.

The introductory word is a special breed. It is called a RELATIVE PRONOUN, and its function is double-barreled. It introduces the subordinate clause and acts as the subject of the clause. There are only a few relative pronouns in our language. They are:

> who
> whom
> which
> that
> what
> where

A general rule is that the relative pronoun usually introduces an **adjective clause,** a dependent clause which modifies a noun or a pronoun in the independent clause. Let us, once again, turn to the diagram:

The man who was in the room *awoke when the sun rose.*

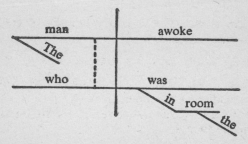

Note that the entire clause modifies the one noun *man;* this relationship is indicated by the connecting line. Then the clause is diagramed as though it were a sentence in itself.

The **adverbial clause** follows this same general pattern

except that its adverbial function is to modify verbs, adjectives or adverbs. The word which introduces the adverbial clause is called a **subordinating conjunction.** The most noteworthy of the many such conjunctions is the word *when* or its alternate *whenever.* The sight of these words which introduce clauses **always relating to time,** is a sure sign of an **adverbial construction.**

Here is the diagram.

. . . awoke when the sun rose.

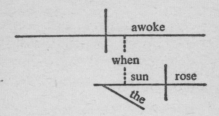

Again the clause modifies a **single word** in the main clause.

Let us look at the diagram of this entire sentence.

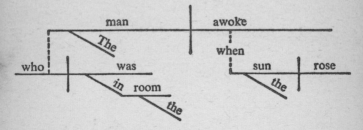

The diagram illustrates very sharply the dependent nature of the two clauses. Sever the connecting links and the clauses float free and meaningless, while the main clause *The man awoke* stands steady as Gibraltar.

We now turn to a truth as applicable to grammar as to any other aspect of life: that into each generalization some exception must fall. We have said that most subordinate clauses and phrases play the role of adjective or adverbial modifiers. There are cases, however, when such constructions act as nouns; that is, they may be subjects or objects within a sentence. Let us examine an example:

"In the spring" is a phrase.

If we diagram that sentence, what is the subject?

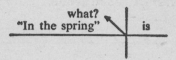

In effect, the entire phrase is the subject of the sentence, thus acting as noun and called a NOUN PHRASE. Obviously this is a rather special and relatively rare use of the phrase, but it does occur.

Or, to take another example:

He shouted, "On the target!"

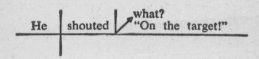

The quotation, a phrase, becomes the object of the verb, receiving the action of *shouted,* and is therefore a noun phrase.

There are also examples among the clauses:

He said that he lied!

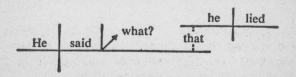

Here the entire clause receives the action of the verb *said* and becomes its object.

What is right is right.

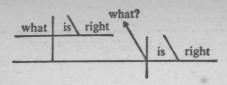

The subject of the sentence is the whole clause *What is right,* a noun clause.

EXERCISE 8.

A. Underline each adjective clause and indicate the word it modifies. (Answers on p. 135.)

1. The film that was produced abroad won the award.
2. If the stars who made it can work together again, they'll win again.
3. The prize that everyone covets is the gold statuette which gleams in its case.
4. I admire the man who works behind the scenes.
5. But will they ever give an award to the viewer who patiently sits through the poorer films?

B. Pick out the adverbial clauses in the following. (Answers on p. 135.)

1. When the moon shone bright, he crept to the corral.
2. The horses grazed quietly while he approached.
3. He froze whenever he heard them whinnying.
4. If they smelled him, they would panic.
5. He ran suddenly when a great stallion approached.

IV. THE SENTENCE (2)

A diet of hamburgers may become dull and boring. A diet of steak may become monotonous. A diet of whipped cream may become fattening and tiresome. A diet of vegetables may become dull. A diet of any single food or unchanging combination of foods may become monotonous. And a reading diet of sentences such as the foregoing is guaranteed to make a reader forswear books and revert to television exclusively.

Note, however, that each sentence above is soundly and grammatically constructed. Note how clear the meaning is in each case. The subject appears first and then come the verb and the completed thought. Variety is missing, the spice that comes from personal interpretation, from nuance of meaning, which is what is involved in good writers' style and maturity of expression. **Sentence variety** is one of the surest ways to help achieve an individual style. Let us examine some different types of sentences which may be used to make writing interesting, varied and distinctively our own.

There are three kinds of sentences: SIMPLE, COMPOUND and COMPLEX.

The simple sentence is easy to recognize. It contains a subject, a verb and a single thought or idea. Certain variations are possible, however, even within this apparently rigid framework. For instance:

Man o' War and Sea Biscuit ran swiftly.

What would you identify as the subject of this sentence? *Man o' War* and *Sea Biscuit* are two nouns connected by the conjunction *and*. This is called a **compound subject** and would be diagrammed as follows:

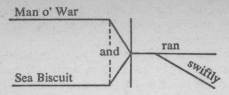

Let us examine another variation:

A steeplechaser runs and jumps.

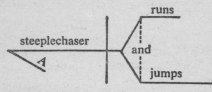

In this case the simple sentence contains a **compound verb**: *runs* and *jumps,* connected by the conjunction *and.* The next step is logical enough.

A steeplechaser and a hurdler run and jump.

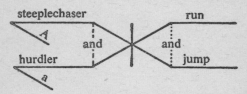

You have a simple sentence with a compound subject, *steeplechaser and hurdler,* and a compound verb, *run and jump.*

Even within the relatively uninspired guise of the simple sentence we can achieve great flexibility.

The next type of sentence, in order of complexity, is the compound. Such a sentence is merely two simple sentences linked by a coordinating conjunction. Or as it is formally defined: **A compound sentence consists of two equal, independent clauses joined by a coordinating conjunction.** Several terms in this definition deserve special regard. The word *equal* implies that neither clause is more important than the other; in other words, that the order of the clauses could be changed without any alteration in the significance of the sentence.

Calling the clauses "independent" is merely another way of saying that each contains subject, verb and completed thought and could stand as a separate sentence. The use of the coordinating conjunction is another means of illustrating the equality of the clauses. Were one of them subordinate to the other, the connecting term might well be a subordinating conjunction, a designation which immediately establishes dependency.

Let us return to our race-track example. (Since we have but a nodding acquaintance with the runners, trotters and jumpers, please forgive any misidentification!)

Equipoise galloped, and Gray Ghost trotted.

What makes this a compound sentence? Each unit, before and after the *and,* is a complete sentence.

(1) *Equipoise*—noun (subject)
    galloped —verb

                and

(2) *Gray Ghost*—noun (subject)
    trotted   —verb

We may reverse the order of the clauses without disturbing the meaning of the sentence:

Gray Ghost trotted, and Equipoise galloped.

Thus we see illustrated the significance of the "equal, independent" status of the clauses.

Diagramed, the compound sentence appears as follows:

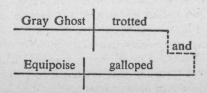

If we omit any aspect of the independent nature of the clauses, the sentence would no longer be compound and its meaning would be radically changed.

In *Gray Ghost trotted and galloped,* we have a completely different sentence. It is now a simple sentence with a compound verb.

At this point we may turn our attention to an associated problem, the proper punctuation of the compound sentence. Punctuation, we recall, is a convenient tool used to help achieve clarity and understanding. There is nothing sacrosanct or unchanging about "rules" of punctuation, and relatively few are constant. The one involving compound sentences is justified principally because it does help us to avoid misreading. The rule is simply: **Place a comma before the coordinating conjunction separating the clauses of a compound sentence.**

Diagrammatically the rule would look like this:

clause (, conjunction) clause

The one variation permitted is the substitution of a semicolon for the conjunction:

clause; clause

The most complicated sentence form, and the richest in potentialities, is the complex sentence. By definition, it consists of **one principal (main or independent) clause and one or more subordinate (dependent) clauses, linked by relative pronouns or conjunctions.** Remember the image of the locomotive, independent and moved by its own power, plus the cars, dependent and without movement unless attached to the independent construction? In a complex sentence, for the most part the dependent clauses will be modifiers in use, **therefore either adjective or adverbial clauses.** Like their namesakes, they will be used in connection with nouns, pronouns, verbs, adjectives or adverbs which they modify. The chief features identifying these clauses will be the relative pronouns *who, whom, that, which* for adjective clauses; the subordinating conjunctions *when, since, if, because* and many others are used for the adverbial clauses. Let us take one example:

The man who drove the car saw my father.

The word *who* is followed by a verb, *drove*. The gong rings; RELATIVE PRONOUN + VERB = CLAUSE. Further, which *man* saw my father? The *man who drove the car*. The group of words . . . *who drove the car* contains a subject, *who*, plus the verb *is*, but it cannot stand alone. Hence, it is a subordinate clause. It modifies a noun; hence, it is an adjective clause. Diagram it:

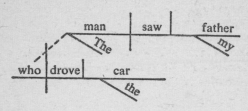

He laughed when he saw the monkey.

Again the gong sounds; *when* is a subordinating conjunction. It introduces a group of words containing a subject, *he*, and a verb, *saw*. This cluster of words cannot stand alone and is a subordinate clause. It answers the question *When?* after a verb. Hence, it is adverbial. Here is the diagram:

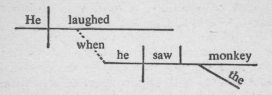

In each case, note how the first clause can stand independently while the modifying clauses cannot. This is the core of the complex sentence.

When the sun shines, the man who
complains, complains alone.

This is rather complicated, yet the logic of the diagram can reduce it to simple terms:

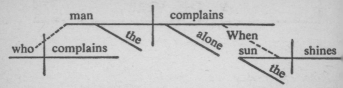

Which man? The one *who complains*—adjective clause
Complains how? *alone*—adverb
Complains when? *When the sun shines*—adverbial clause

EXERCISE 9. Sense and Sentences

A. Can you identify correctly the different types of sentences in the following paragraph? Label each sentence S—simple; Co—compound; Cx—complex; I—interrogative; or Inc—incomplete. (Answers on p. 135-6.)

Grammar is not of earthshaking importance. Not really. One may even be a very good friend of someone who speaks and writes ungrammatically. Jimmy may grunt and Johnny may orate. They may still be friends. But let us ask ourselves this question. Is there anything wrong with using the language correctly? Would you be satisfied with teaching your son to wash the car fairly well? Are you content with less than perfection when your wife parks the car? Language is really less complicated than the inside of a TV set. If you can understand and repair the one, you certainly should be able to handle the other.

B. And now for a little tricky diagraming (this is all just for fun, but it will assist you in gaining an understanding of our grammar). (Answers on p. 136.)

1. The lamb followed wherever Mary led.
2. Mary was a child who knew lambs.
3. This was a lamb that needed education.
4. When it bleated, it bleated incorrectly.
5. While the lamb followed, Mary led it to school.

V. THE VERB

Rules are made to be broken!
There's an exception to every rule!
Throw away the book!

How frequently have we heard this litany; how often have we eased our consciences by rubbing on this verbal palm? It is interesting to observe, however, that in the very statement of these declarations of independence, certain rules are faithfully adhered to. Notice that we don't say:

> *Rules* **is** *made to be* **broke!**

or

> **There's exceptions** *to every rule!*

or

> *Throw the books* **aways!**

And I'm inclined to think that if these slogans were couched in incorrect English, most of their effectiveness would be lost.

So it is with our language and its grammar. While at present there are few grammatical absolutes, and within the foreseeable future these may be further reduced, there are valid reasons for accepting and following the rules.

First, there is the simple pleasure which comes from being right. Suffice it to say that occasionally one ought to answer the challenge "Why do we have to do it this way?" with a flat "Because it's right!" It feels good.

There is a second reason for speaking and writing correctly. Language is capable of both incisive clarity and the broadest ambiguity. There is an intimate connection between the correct use of word, phrase and grammatical rule, and sureness of comprehension. In conversation, listen to the frequent repetitions of "What I mean is . . ." and "Y'know what I mean . . ." and you are witnessing the difficulties of people trying to make themselves understood.

Let us approach this problem through the verbs. The verbs, which are central to meaning, have several facets from which false light may be reflected. We shall begin by considering tense, **the changing form of the verb by which time is indicated.**

Each verb has three principal parts: present, past, past participle. The past participle is always formed with the use of *have, has* or *had* as an auxiliary or helping verb. Here is an example of the three chief parts of the verb *to help*.

NOTE: The root or infinitive of virtually all English verbs is formed by using the preposition *to* with the verb itself.

	PRESENT	PAST	PAST PARTICIPLE
SINGULAR:	*I help*	*helped*	*have-had helped*
	you help	*helped*	*have-had helped*
	he, she, it helps	*helped*	*has-had helped*
PLURAL:	*we help*	*helped*	*have-had helped*
	you help	*helped*	*have-had helped*
	they help	*helped*	*have-had helped*

The verb *to help* is a sample of the **regular verb.** The past tense and the past participial form are arrived at by the simple addition of *-ed* to the root. Other regular verbs are: *smile-smiled-smiled; watch-watched-watched; struggle-struggled-struggled.* In the last it was necessary only to add *d.* As is common in English grammar, the regular forms are not necessarily the predominant ones. Many verbs form their past tense by undergoing complete transformation. For instance, *see-saw-seen; grow-grew-grown; is-was-been.*

Here are some of the most frequently misused irregular verbs. Learning them is a matter of memorizing, visualizing and using.

PRESENT	PAST	PAST PARTICIPLE (have, has, had)
bear (to carry)	*bore*	*borne*
begin	*began*	*begun*
bite	*bit*	*bitten*
blow	*blew*	*blown*
break	*broke*	*broken*
bring	*brought*	*brought*
burst	*burst*	*burst*
choose	*chose*	*chosen*
dive	*dived (dove)*	*dived*
do	*did*	*done*
drink	*drank*	*drunk*
fall	*fell*	*fallen*
fly	*flew*	*flown*
forget	*forgot*	*forgotten*
freeze	*froze*	*frozen*
get	*got*	*got (gotten)*
give	*gave*	*given*
grow	*grew*	*grown*
hang (a person)	*hanged*	*hanged*
hang (an object)	*hung*	*hung*
know	*knew*	*known*
lay (to put)	*laid*	*laid*
lead (to guide)	*led*	*led*
lend	*lent*	*lent*
lie (recline)	*lay*	*lain*
lie (tell untruth)	*lied*	*lied*
ride	*rode*	*ridden*
ring	*rang*	*rung*
run	*ran*	*run*
shine (the sun)	*shone*	*shone*
shine (polish)	*shined*	*shined*
show	*showed*	*shown*
sing	*sang*	*sung*
sink	*sank*	*sunk*
sit	*sat*	*sut*

PRESENT	PAST	PAST PARTICIPLE
		(have, has, had)
steal	*stole*	*stolen*
swim	*swam*	*swum*
take	*took*	*taken*
throw	*threw*	*thrown*
write	*wrote*	*written*

The principal parts of the verbs are of interest and importance not only for themselves but because of the use made of them in producing various tenses. Of these there are five particularly important tenses: the PRESENT, PAST, PRESENT PERFECT, PAST PERFECT and FUTURE. Because these are of great concern to anyone who wishes to develop accuracy of expression, and because there is frequent confusion about them, we shall proceed slowly and step by step in our analysis.

The present: This tense has two main functions: to indicate action or state of being at the present time; or to show an action or state of being which is characteristically true. Present tense is often modified to indicate an action that is proceeding as you speak. Note . . . *action that is proceeding.* . . . This is called the **present progressive tense,** formed by adding a helping verb, *is-are-am,* and the *-ing* form of the verb.

What are you doing? *I* **am writing** *a book.*
Present progressive tense
Where are you? *I* **am** *here.*
Simple present tense
What do you do after showering? *I* **powder** *myself.*
Action characteristically true

It is frequently and correctly remarked that in English we use the progressive form widely where, in other languages, the simple present would suffice. Thus, to the question, *What are you doing?* we reply, *I* **am riding** *a horse.* We do not say *I ride a horse.* Nor do we say *I speak to him* or *I go to the store.* We say, instead, *I am speaking to him* and *I am going to the store.* This usage becomes part of the idiom of speech which makes each language unique and gives flavor and variety to communication. This, also, makes artistic and true translation from language to language a formidable task.

The past: This tense is used to indicate an action or condition which took place or existed at a stated and usually limited time in the past. Think in terms of the rapid opening and closing of a door, an open-shut action completed.

I saw him yesterday.

It might have been a glimpse or a conversation, but the action is completed.

Rome **fell** *beneath the weight of its own corruption.*

The fall took some time, though at a distance of two thousand years the action seems abrupt.

I **spoke** *to him a moment ago.*

Five minutes ago he dashed out, but I managed to have a word with him.

The present perfect: This tense is a combination involving a use of *have-has* plus the past participle of the verb. It indicates an action commenced in the past and carried into the present, or an action begun and completed during some span of time but at no specific time in the past. This door has opened and closed more slowly. Visualize it this way:

I **have worked** *here for three months.*

Past	Present
have	worked →

The sentence indicates that the subject is still working here.

I **have completed** *the job.*

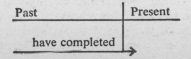

The indication here is that the job has **just been completed** at a time very close to the present—a recent past.

The past perfect: This tense permits some rather subtle shadings of meaning. It is used in conjunction with the simple past tense and indicates **a sequence of several actions in the past** in which one action has taken place before the other. When the helping verb is employed, and it must be, the *had* form is called for. The picture of the past perfect tense is:

He **had gone** *before I* **reached** *the office.*

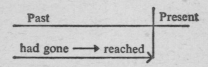

Notice that two actions were performed in the past, but the *had gone* occurred before the *reached,* and the past perfect tense expresses this relationship.

I **had warned** *him before he* **left.**

Which action took place first? The warning did.
Which followed? The leaving did.
Thus:

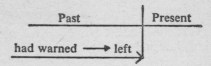

The future: This tense, as its name implies, reveals what is to be. It is formed by making use of the regular form of the verb, preceded by *shall* or *will.*

I shall go	*We shall go*
You will go	*You will go*
He, she, it will go	*They will go*

This is the construction of all verbs in the future tense.

EXERCISE 10. Tenses, Anyone?

Choose the correct tense from those offered. (Visualize which action **preceded** which other action!) (Answers on p. 137.)

1. Before Columbus (journeyed, had journeyed) across the sea, people (had imagined, imagined) that a voyager would topple off the edge of the earth.

2. The Genoese navigator (had pleaded, pleaded) vainly with many monarchs before Isabella (granted, had granted) him an audience.

3. We may assume that the Queen (argued, had argued) strongly with Ferdinand before he (decided, had decided) to give his approval.

4. Notice that he (gave, had given) his approval only after the Queen (had given, gave) her jewels.

5. However, Columbus' voyages (released, have released, had released) people from a superstition which (held, had held, has held) them for centuries.

6. I (had, have) just completed reading about this when I (have heard, had heard, heard) about Colonel Glenn's flight.

7. I thought: "We (have entered, entered, had entered) a new stage of exploration."

8. The great line of brave pioneers (has not ended, did not end, had not ended).

There is, of course, much more to the mastery of verbs than the matter of tenses. There is also the agreement of the verb with its subject in terms of number. We use a different form of the verb when we speak of several people who do something rather than one person doing something.

The pattern of forming the singular and plural of verbs is interesting and simple. The one slight complication enters with an element referred to as **person.** Every verb may be broken down—**conjugated** is the formal term—

into various parts according to the precise meaning desired. Let us examine this closely:

		PRESENT	PAST
SINGULAR:	*I*—first person	*am*	*was*
	you—second person	*are*	*were*
	he, she, it—third person	*is*	*was*
PLURAL:	*we*—first person	*are*	*were*
	you—second person	*are*	*were*
	they—third person	*are*	*were*

In the verb *to be* there is no variation in the plural forms. Let us search further:

		PRESENT	PAST
SINGULAR:	*I*—first person	*argue*	*argued*
	you—second person	*argue*	*argued*
	he, she, it—third person	*argues*	*argued*
PLURAL:	*we*—first person	*argue*	*argued*
	you—second person	*argue*	*argued*
	they—third person	*argue*	*argued*

Before arriving at any conclusions, let us conjugate still one more verb:

		PRESENT	PAST
SINGULAR:	*I*—first person	*have*	*had*
	you—second person	*have*	*had*
	he, she, it—third person	*has*	*had*
PLURAL:	*we*—first person	*have*	*had*
	you—second person	*have*	*had*
	they—third person	*have*	*had*

We may generalize on the basis of those three examples: **The third person singular of verbs is usually formed by adding -s or -es to the verb; the plural form remains the same for all persons.**

The problem now remains one of simply fitting together the proper subjects and verbs in terms of number (singular or plural). Occasional words do provide a challenge.

Either Tom or Harry (are, is) *in charge.*
Problem: Shall we say *are* or *is?*
Neither Jerry, John nor Jephthah (are, is) *my friend.*
Again, is it *is* or is it *are?*

The rule is that *either* and *neither* generally take the **singular form of the verb.** In attempting to determine the correct usage, put the word *one* immediately after the *either* or *neither.* If it makes sense, then the verb is singular:

> *Either (one) . . .* is *in charge.*
> *Neither (one) . . .* is *my friend.*

The exceptions to the *"either-neither* = singular" rule are few, and present no formidable challenge.

> *Neither* we *nor* they (is, are) *happy about it.*

In this case, since both subject elements, *we* and *they,* are plural, the verb itself must be plural.

> *Neither* **Mark and David** *nor* **Joan and Theresa** (is, are) *going to the dance.*

Again the compound subjects call for the plural. The verb must be *are.*

The next case is a little more intriguing, however.

> *Either the teacher or his students* (is, are) *correct.*

The problem here is clear. *Teacher* is singular and should take *is. Students* is plural and should take *are.* No verb form in English serves both singular and plural.

The solution is somewhat arbitrary, but logical: **Use the verb form called for by the nearer subject.** *Students* is nearer to the verb; therefore we say *are.*

> *Either the teacher or the* **students** **are** *correct.*

Should the order of the terms be reversed, it would become:

> *Either the students or the* **teacher is** *correct.*

Though this usage is grammatically correct, it is somewhat awkward. It might be better to avoid the difficulty by writing the sentence thus:

Either the students are, or the teacher is, correct.

or

Either the students are correct, or the teacher is.

A somewhat similar cause for concern is generated in dealing with such words as *everyone, everybody, anyone* and *anybody*. These terms have a mixed nature; they seem to be both plural and singular.

Everyone (**do, does**) *as well as possible.*

Well, now, the concept is certainly plural, but the grammatical function is singular:

Everyone **does** *as well as possible.*
Everybody (**want, wants**) *to come along.*

Again:

Everybody **wants** *to come along.*

The rule is that these words, though plural in intention, govern singular verbs. But there is a further problem.

Everyone (**minds, mind**) (**their, his**) *own business.*

We have mastered the verb; we know it should be *minds,* the singular. But what about the pronoun? *Their* or *his?* If "everyone" is treated as singular and takes a singular verb, then the possessive pronouns must be singular as well:

Everyone **minds his** *own business.*

We see now that these special words, though plural in intent, nevertheless demand singular verb and possessive pronoun. And we can, I think, accept this readily enough. But why, in each case, do we use the **masculine possessive pronoun** *his?* What about the ladies?

Even in grammar it appears to be a man's world. We could say, *Everyone minds* **his or her own business.** But that is very awkward. If we said *Everyone minds* **her** *own business,* the only accepted interpretation would be that we were speaking of an all-female assemblage. In such cases the male *his* is used to include all people, male and female together, as well as all-male groups.

EXERCISE 11.
Decision! Decisions! Singular or Plural?

(Answers on p. 137-8.)

1. Either red roses or white ones (are, is) suitable.
2. At one time, in England, neither red nor white rose (was, were) without political significance.
3. It was either the House of York or that of Lancaster which (were, was) represented by the White Rose. [Actually, it was York!]
4. Oddly enough, either a flower or some other symbol (are, is) frequently associated with history.
5. Either the bald eagle or the fifty stars (is, are) representative of the United States.
6. Neither Iceland nor Finland (has, have) a symbolic animal, as far as I know.
7. Neither the teacher nor the students in the class (are, is) able to keep abreast of national colors.
8. Either red, white and blue or red, orange and green (is, are) colors frequently seen in flags.
9. Neither the lion and the unicorn nor the eagle (represent, represents) France.
10. Neither Parliament, Diet nor King now (rule, rules) in the United States.

VI. COMMON PROBLEMS

Steaming proudly up New York Harbor, the Statue of Liberty could be seen clearly.

The lady was speaking to the policeman with the bright polka-dot dress.

What an awe-inspiring experience the first sentence describes, and how much like science fiction!

And how droll is the sight the second sentence conjures up!

I think we have little difficulty in understanding what is **really meant** in each case. But why do we not say what we **really mean** instead of asking the reader or listener to interpret for us?

Since a modifier usually precedes or closely follows the word it modifies, the first sentence above tells us that the Statue of Liberty was *steaming proudly up New York Harbor.* This is an example of what is termed a DANGLING PARTICIPLE. The phrase introduced by the *-ing* form of the verb (participle) is left dangling so that it appears to modify what in fact it does not. Let us first diagram this erroneous sentence:

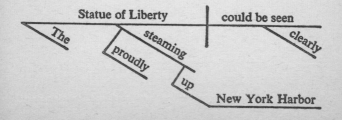

The true meaning is probably, *From the* **ship,** *steaming proudly up New York Harbor, the Statue of Liberty could be seen clearly*. The corrected sentence would therefore appear in the diagram like this:

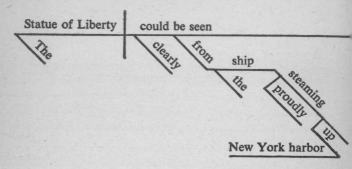

The simplest way to avoid this type of error is, clearly, to provide the word which must, **logically,** be modified by the phrase.

Thus:

Running madly down the street, the overturned carriage tripped me up.

Question: Who was running madly? Hardly the overturned carriage!

Correction:

Running madly down the street, **I** *was tripped by the overturned carriage*.

Thus the participial phrase modifies *I*, not *carriage*. And the sentence then makes sense.

Let us now return for a glimpse of our dazzlingly clad policeman. Assuming normal circumstances, it is logical to think that the lady *with the bright polka-dot dress* was speaking to a policeman. This sentence demonstrates the use of a **misplaced modifier.** The adjective phrase *with the bright polka-dot dress* modifies *lady* and should, therefore, be placed next to that word. Here is the picture:

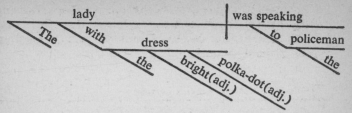

We would reconstruct the sentence to read as follows:

The lady with the bright polka-dot dress was speaking to the policeman.

In all likelihood we would not be led astray by such poorly written, or spoken, sentences as those at the beginning of the chapter. But doing things correctly can be a guarantee against misunderstanding.

Another example somewhat humorously reinforces the point:

John galloped off on a superb steed with a leg in a cast.

Question: Who wore the cast? It is not likely that it was the horse.

Correction:

John, with his leg in a cast, galloped off on a superb steed.

Now the adjective phrase follows directly the word it modifies, making sense because it adheres to the rule.

One meets another family of errors even more frequently than the preceding. To correct them, and to stick to the correct usage in daily speech, calls for a certain amount of moral courage. How do you plead to the charge of saying these?

> *He's bigger than me.*

or

> *I think these are more exciting than them.*

or

> *They have more men than us.*

The company which pleads guilty as charged is large indeed. Yet the reason for the error is clear to see and the correction is as easy to understand and to accomplish.

When we see the preposition *than,* we believe that if it is followed by a pronoun that pronoun must be in the *objective* case: *me, him, her, us, them.* The rule, however, indicates that if what follows *than* directly contains a **verb concept,** then the pronoun must be in the **nominative** case, as the subject of the unexpressed verb.

Let us examine the samples. What do we mean in case number one? *He's bigger than (I am big)* or, more simply, *He's bigger than (I am).* Therefore, the correct usage is:

He's bigger than **I.**

Look at number two. *I think these are more exciting than (they are).* Hence,

I think these are more exciting than **they.**

And finally, *They have more men than (we have).* So, *They have more men than* **we.**

One of the thorniest problems of proper usage comes from another aspect of the nominative-objective case problem. Picture this traditional situation: a door to a room, a tenant within, a visitor without:

VISITOR: *Knock, knock.*
TENANT: *Who's there?*
VISITOR: *It's . . .* (**I, me**).

(Let us ignore the spoilsport who dodges his responsibility and answers with his name!)

Tradition, sanctioned by time and authority, demands the nominative case after the copulative (state-of-being) verb. Thus, *It's* **I** or *It is* **I.**

To the consternation of the purists, such current authorities as the New York State Board of Regents, Sir Winston Churchill and many millions of users of the language accept *It's* **me.** Their argument is based, not on points of grammatical law nor of academic approval, but on grounds of widespread usage and the changing trends of language. Oddly enough, there is no consistent adherence to the changed usage. No authority states that *It's* **him** or *It's*

them are the preferable forms. This inconsistency strengthens the positions of the old guard, with Fowler's *Modern English Usage* at its head, which demands *It's* **I** as well as *It's* **we** and *It is* **they.**

The resolution of this problem is not perfect, but it is sufficient for general guidance. Formal usage in written or spoken language still requires the nominative after a state-of-being verb: *It is* **I.** Colloquial, everyday speech permits *It's* **me.**

But the rules governing what follows are somewhat more rigid than what has gone before. The expression *I feel* **badly** *about it* is grammatically wrong. The error can be demonstrated logically. The word *badly* is an adverb and modifies (describes) the verb *feel.* It would therefore appear to describe **the manner in which the feeling is done.** As though one were saying that his performance of the **function of feeling,** in the dark, or as a blind person, was inadequate. What we actually mean is: *I feel* **unhappy,** or **sad,** or **upset,** *about it.* In that case we use an **adjective** called a **predicate adjective,** to **complete the verb,** not to modify it.

To test which to use, simply substitute a part of the verb *to be* for the verb involved: *feel, look, seem, smell.* The final term is then the predicate adjective. If you cannot make such a substitution, you probably have an action verb which calls for an adverb as a modifier.

Let us take a few examples:

> *The rose smelled* (**sweet, sweetly**)**.**

Make the test. Can you legitimately substitute *was?*

The rose **was**—yes, it makes sense. The completed sentence would then be, *The rose* **was sweet.** *Sweet* is a predicate adjective after the state-of-being verb *smelled,* as in *The rose* **smelled sweet.**

But *smelled* is not always a state-of-being verb:

> *The Indian guide* **smelled warily.**

If you substitute *was* here, you change the meaning of the sentence completely. You do not mean *The Indian guide* was warily; you are describing the manner in which he performed a certain physical action. Hence, you use the adverb, because the verb is an action verb.

In connection with this choice of adverb or adjective, there are certain exceptions to the rule. The idiomatic phrase about physical health illustrates one such exception. We say *I feel* **well** or *I am* **well** or *I am* **ill** in response to questions about our physical condition. The phrases *I feel* **good** and *I am* **good** have a very different meaning. The latter refers to moral rather than physical welfare. In general, however, the rule stands.

EXERCISE 12. What's the Usage?

A. Correct the following sentences by rearranging the modifiers where necessary, and removing the dangling elements. (Answers on p. 138.)

1. The fire siren, with his radio turned on full blast, could not be heard.
2. Looking into the rearview mirror there was a huge, roaring hook-and-ladder truck.
3. With a shout of fear the car swerved toward the sidewalk.
4. The driver wiped his brow with the firemen yelling at him as they drove past.
5. Pulling away from the curb slowly you could see that he had learned his lesson.

B. Choose the correct usage. (Answers on p. 138.)

1. He tasted the food (careful, carefully).
2. That was because the soup had not tasted (well, good).
3. Obviously, it was (they, them) who had made up the recipe.
4. While the meal smelled (well, good), it did not look (good, well.)
5. He tasted (carefully, careful) and smelled (good, well) before he left the table.

VII. PUNCTUATION

When mankind passed through the grunt-and-groan stage and language had been invented everyone was happy communication has been established they said and now we can understand each other then writing was developed so that words could be given some durability how wonderful everyone exclaimed now we can read and write but then they began to have difficulty understanding what was written down because everything seemed to run together how confusing they complained so they invented sentences and phrases and clauses and punctuation. "Now," they stated gleefully, "we can set our thoughts down, read them and understand just what is meant."

Oversimplification? Yes! But one major point becomes clear. Punctuation is not a set of unyielding rules into whose mold language must be crammed. Rather it is a series of devices designed, principally, to promote clarity, prevent misunderstanding and develop to a maximum degree the strength and impact of the written language.

The simplest marks to understand and use are those of **terminal** punctuation. There are three such marks: the PERIOD, the QUESTION MARK and the EXCLAMATION POINT.

All simple statements, or declarative sentences, have a period as a terminal mark. In almost all the reading you do, the period is the most commonly used final punctuation mark.

The question mark is the sign of inquiry and may be used at the end of a long, involved question or immediately after a short, sharp questioning word. **How?** Just so!

The last of the three terminal marks is the exclamation point, the most dramatic sign of the language. All strong emotions—anger, surprise, shock, defiance—are indicated by this bold mark. In formal writing, however, we avoid the advertising- and pulp-inspired multiplication of exclamation points for added effect. The cry *Help!* is no more effective with four or five punctuation marks than with one!

These three forms of punctuation actually cause little difficulty. The **internal** punctuation marks, the signs which guide us through variations of sentence structure, changes of direction in thought and nuances of meaning, are the ones that create problems. The chief cause of concern is usually the proper use of the COMMA.

There are only a few hard and fast rules for use of the comma. Where no specific rule is involved, we judge solely in terms of clarity of understanding. Will the comma help make the meaning clear? If so, use it! Is it unnecessary for clarity? Then dispense with it!

Now to some of the rules. First, the comma is used to separate words in a series.

The fisherman bought bait, tackle, leads and lunch.

The same principle holds in relation to series of phrases:

The plane circled the field, zoomed through an open hangar, roared under the bridge and disappeared into the clouds.

The general rule, then, would be: **The comma is used to separate words or phrases in a series.**

Though this appears to be a fairly ironclad regulation, there is a certain degree of latitude in its application. In the case of the last pair in a series either of words or phrases, where the word *and* is used, the comma is optional. You may use it or omit it, as you think best. It is good form, however, to be consistent in any one piece of writing. If you omit the comma in one place, omit it throughout. If you use it once, continue the practice all the way.

. . . *tackle, leads, and lunch,* or . . . *tackle, leads and lunch.*

. . . *roared under the bridge, and disappeared into the*

clouds, or . . . *roared under the bridge and disappeared into the clouds.*

Another generally accepted rule for the comma is: **Place a comma before the conjunction in a compound sentence.** (Remember that our definition of a compound sentence states that it consists of two independent clauses joined by a coordinating conjunction.) For an example, we have this:

Francis Marion was an American guerrilla **leader, and** *the British called him "The Swamp Fox."*

The picture to bear in mind is COMMA + CONJUNCTION.

John Thomas leaped seven **feet, but** *he did not retain the championship.*

Again, COMMA + CONJUNCTION.

In punctuating the compound sentence, there is one possible alternative. One can use a semicolon instead of the COMMA + CONJUNCTION combination. Let us repeat the two previous sample sentences punctuated that way:

Francis Marion was an American guerrilla leader; the British called him "The Swamp Fox."

John Thomas leaped seven feet; he did not retain the championship.

NOTE: To write any of the above sentences **using only a comma to separate the clauses is to commit an offense against good writing: a run-on** sentence!

We all have, I'm sure, noticed that English, while it is a language of great directness, can be, in addition, used to confound understanding.

Please observe that foregoing sentence carefully. Reread it, this time omitting all absolutely nonessential material. What should emerge is:

"We all have noticed that English can be used to confound understanding."

That is the core of meaning in this sentence. Well, then, what of the rest?—*I'm sure; while it is a language of great directness;* and *in addition!* These are all interjected elements set off from the rest of the sentence by commas.

Each of these little phrases adds something to the complete meaning. It may be a personal touch, or a slight filling in of background information. All of this will, **of course** (note that small much-used space-filler!), have some significance in the entire sentence, but it will not be indispensable. And all such elements, sometimes called parenthetical expressions, are walled off from the rest of the sentence by commas, one before and one immediately following the expression.

This "setting off" can supply an excellent device for judging whether or not the phrase is essential. Visualize the commas as ice tongs poised to lift the phrase out of the sentence. If the **basic meaning** of the sentence is not changed by removing the smaller unit, then the latter is not essential, and should be set off by commas. If, on the other hand, the meaning would be radically changed, the commas are omitted, because the expression is essential.

Almost all such words and phrases as *however, of course, I think, you see,* when thrust into the middle of a sentence, are interjective or parenthetical in intent. They are, therefore, set apart by commas. From this emerges the rule: **Use commas to set off all interjected and parenthetical elements.**

RULE: **Commas are used to set off nouns in direct address.**

When we ask a question, and, in the course of it, use the name of the person we are speaking to, his name becomes a noun in direct address.

Frank, *do you really want to become a singer?*

Frank, a noun in direct address, is set off by a comma.

Perhaps we are not asking a question but only making a simple comment:

I can't see, **Miles,** *why you don't ask her yourself!*

Miles is a noun in direct address, and is set off by commas.

Maybe you don't know the name of the person to whom you are speaking:

I beg your pardon, sir, but can you tell me which end has the filter?

There are two ways to remember this use of the comma. First, simply remember the definition and function of the noun in direct address. Second, visualize the noun in direct address as another example of a parenthetical phrase—and, therefore, to be set off by commas.

The next recommendation for use of the comma, a recommendation rather than a rigid regulation, is based upon a desire for clarity. **If there is an unusually long introductory phrase or clause standing before the subject of the sentence,** it should be set off by a comma. Notice the previous sentence itself. We have a long adverbial clause coming before the main clause and it is set off by a comma. This rule can also be divided into two parts: (1) If the introductory element is a long phrase, the comma **may** be used; (2) if the introductory element is a clause, the comma **should** be used.

The remaining few points about the comma involve routine, mechanical matters which, once learned, should be put into practice and so become part of us.

1. The comma is used to separate the names of towns, boroughs, cities, states and countries:

> *Brooklyn 34, New York, U.S.A.*
> *Maspeth 78, Queens, New York*

2. The comma is used to separate the day and month from the year in a date:

> *June 14, 1961*
> *May 1, 1921*

An occasional variation is this form, which obviates the necessity for any punctuation:

> *22 March 1946*
> *20 February 1949*

Of course, this form has not yet been accepted as part of normal business practice, and it would probably be frowned upon.

3. The comma is used after the salutation in a friendly letter:

Dear Mario,

4. The comma is always used after the close of all letters, friendly or formal:

Sincerely yours,
Your pal,

The SEMICOLON is sometimes referred to as a "strong" comma or a "weak" period. Its uses are definite and limited.

First, **the semicolon may be used instead of the** COMMA $+$ CONJUNCTION **in a compound sentence.** We have already seen this use in our discussion of the comma in the compound sentence.

Second, **the semicolon is used to break up a sequence of series of words or phrases.** Thus:

On the first floor he purchased ties, shirts and socks; on the second, trousers, jackets and hats; and on the third, blankets, sheets and pillowcases.

Perhaps the most stilted and formal of the marks of punctuation is the COLON. This solemn mark is rarely used. The colon is used in the formal salutation of formal correspondence:

Dear Mr. President:
Honored Sir:
My Dear Sir:

It is also used after the expressions *as follows* or *the following.*

He spoke as follows: "Gentlemen!"

They saw the following: skyscrapers, ferries, bridges and tenements.

The colon is also employed where the foregoing expressions seem to be implied, as following the word *thus.*

There are a few maverick marks of punctuation which are not very widely used. Among these are the dash, the ellipsis and parentheses.

1. The DASH: The dash is used to indicate an abrupt suspension of the sense, or an unexpected turn of

thought; it is used in pairs to set off interpolations which are less incidental to the sentence than those where we would use parentheses.

2. The ELLIPSIS: this sign (. . .) is used generally in quotations, when we leave out some words or phrases. "I regret . . . for my country."

3. PARENTHESES: used always as a pair, ( ), the parentheses hold explanatory or illustrative material apart from the sentence proper. It is generally wise to use this mark very sparingly.

Much of what we say and much of what we write involves quoting directly what others have said or what we may have read. When we speak directly, we simply say, "John said . . ." or "he told me. . . ." But when we write things down, we must show, in some way, the distinction between our comment and that of others. Therefore, we employ QUOTATION MARKS. There are several rules governing their use:

1. Quotation marks are used to set off direct quotations:

Nathan Hale said, "I regret that I have but one life to lose for my country."

NOTICE: double quotation marks are used before and after the actual words quoted. The period goes inside the final quotation marks.

"I regret," said Nathan Hale, "that I have but one life to lose for my country."

NOTE: the quotation is split into two parts, but it is still *one* sentence. Therefore, quotation marks are around each segment of the quotation. The commas set off the words which are not part of the quotation.

2. Quotation marks are used to set off special or made-up words:

Occasionally one feels the need to use a special term, or one not normally used as he intends it.

We might say of a person that he has a "neither-here-nor-there" sort of personality. We are creating a term; the quotation marks provide the credentials.

Among teenagers the word *boss* has assumed a meaning of high praise, like that once held by *super* and *cool*. Should we want to use this to illustrate a point, we would bracket it with quotation marks in order to give it its special meaning and to indicate that we are not incorporating it directly into our own vocabulary.

3. Quotation marks may be used to set off titles of stories, poems or articles:

Mark Twain wrote "The Notorious Jumping Frog of Calaveras County."

4. A quotation within a quotation is indicated by use of single quotation marks:

He said, "Nathan Hale said, 'I regret. . . .' "

NOTE: The double quote shows what *He* said; the single quote sets off what *Nathan Hale* said. This leads to the final combination of *three* quotation marks.

There is one more important point about quotation marks and dialogue. First, each time there is a change of speaker, a new paragraph is started, even though the spoken interchange may involve only one or two words. Second, if one person's speech goes on for several paragraphs, the opening quotation marks are placed at the beginning of his speech and are repeated at the beginning of each new paragraph. The closing quotation marks, however, are used only at the very end of his last remarks.

Before leaving the subject of punctuation, it is worth emphasizing once again that punctuation is designed to help us express ourselves. When the device becomes master, and man the device, then the charm is wound up and we had better return to the grunt and the groan.

EXERCISE 13.

Go back to the opening sentence of this chapter (p. 59) and rewrite it, using correct punctuation. Remember that when you introduce quotations, you set the quoted statements into paragraphs separated from the rest of the material. (Answer on p. 138.)

VIII. USAGE

Usage is less a matter of rules promulgated by "authorities" than of custom established over the ages. At times custom breeds rules as binding as any textbook decree, but it usually permits change. In this section we shall deal, in alphabetical order, with words, pronunciation and phrases about which there is confusion, doubt and, perhaps, even contradiction.

a, an

These words are called indefinite articles. They are actually used as adjectives, and would be diagrammed as such:

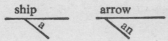

The distinction between them is simple: *a* is used before words beginning with consonants, or with vowels which are pronounced like an initial *y: a house; a ewe; a usual procedure; an* is employed before words beginning with vowels or with initial unvoiced consonants: *an open porch; an honest man* (but, *a historic occasion*).

The word *a* is usually pronounced "uh." To indicate a particular emphasis in speech, it is sometimes pronounced "ay." *There is not* **a** (ay) *single, solitary fact to bear you out*. Which you use is purely a matter of individual choice and personal preference.

accept v. / *except* prep.

The confusion between these two words stems, for the most part, from insufficient distinction in pronunciation. The basic differences, however, are deep-rooted. *Accept* is a verb meaning to take or receive. A good way to remember this is to remember that a verb shows *a*ction. Action begins with an *a* and *accept,* the verb, is spelled with an *a*.

Except is generally used as a preposition introducing a phrase. (Sometimes the word *except* will be used as a verb meaning to omit or leave out. *He agreed to* **except** *his brother from the list*.)

advice n. / *advise* v.
Let us resort to trickery to fix these words in our minds. The first is a **noun**, meaning a suggestion given or guidance offered. If we remember that it contains the noun *ice,* we should be able to recall its spelling.

The word *advise* (pronounced "ad-vize") is the verb, meaning to give a suggestion or offer guidance.

aesthetic adj. / *esthetic* adj. / *ascetic* adj., n.
Aesthetic and *esthetic* are simply two different, accepted spellings of the same word, an adjective meaning pertaining to beauty.

Ascetic, however, is either an adjective or a noun, meaning characterized by neglect or denial of self, or one who practices self-denial: *Hermits are usually* **ascetics.**

affect v. / *effect* n., v.
Again pronunciation is the basis for confusion between two somewhat similar terms. In speech we rarely make a marked distinction between *affect* and *effect*. Where does the difference lie?

Affect is usually a verb meaning to influence, to have an influence upon, to cause, to assume an attitude. Remember it again as verb = action = *a* = **a**ffect.

Effect is most frequently encountered as a noun, meaning result, consequences: *cause and* **e**ffect. (*Effect* also occasionally appears as a verb meaning, to force, to bring about in the face of obstacles as, *They* **effected** *an entrance into the bank*.)

aged v. / *aged* adj.

These two words are, of course, related. The first, pronounced "ayjd," is simply the past participle of the verb *to age: He* **aged** *rapidly; It was* **aged** *in wood; The boy,* **aged** *five, was clever.* The second, pronounced in two syllables, "ay-jed," is an adjective used thus: *He is an* **aged** *man; They felled the* **aged** *oak.*

aggravate v. / *irritate* v.

It is not pronunciation which causes the difficulty here, but a simple confusion of meanings. *Aggravate* is a verb which means to make worse, to intensify. It bears the idea of making worse an already bad situation: *The assassination of the Duke* **aggravated** *the already tense diplomatic situation.*

Irritate is a verb which means to annoy, pester, provoke or exasperate: *Crying children may* **irritate** *a busy, harassed mother; a hungry husband, home from work, may* **aggravate** *her condition.*

ain't

Ain't is a word definitely not accepted in formal, correct usage. It is hardly regarded as proper in normal colloquial usage. It is unfortunate that our language has no convenient and acceptable term to fill this very real need. *Ain't I?* stands for *Am I not? amn't I?* or *aren't I?; I ain't,* for *I am not.* We have the contraction for *You are not: You aren't.* We have contractions for *he, she, it is not: He, she, it isn't.* But there is no contraction for the nominative pronoun *I* and its verb. There was a time when *ain't* was used in fashionable English society; but it is as yet totally unacceptable in American usage.

alley n. / *ally* n., v.

There is really no relationship between these words except careless spelling. *Alley,* pronounced "al-lee," rhymes with *Sally.* It forms its plural by adding *s: Alleys.*

Ally is a verb, pronounced "al-līe," which means to join with, act together with. As a noun the word *ally* means a partner, or a companion in action. The plural is formed by a slight change in form of the word— *allies.*

all right
almost / Almighty / already /
altogether / although / always

It is a strange contradiction which one is forced into when spelling *all right.* Asked to spell one word, one must respond with two: *all right.* But this provides us with a sure device for remembering the spelling: **two words** and therefore **two *l*'s.** The other words, which seem to be members of the same family, are all spelled with one *l* as one word.

allusion n. / illusion n.

Both words are nouns, but here the resemblance ends. An *allusion* means a reference to or a hint about something; an *illusion* is a false impression or a mistaken notion. Thus, in a previous chapter there was an *allusion* to Nathan Hale; in a desert we might see a mirage, which is an optical *illusion.*

altar n. / alter v.

Because they sound identical, these two words cause frequent spelling trouble. *Altar* is a noun meaning a raised place or structure associated with religious sacrifice or worship: *altar* = **a** = *sacrifice.*

Alter is a verb meaning to change or to revise. Remembering the *e*'s may prove of assistance here.

amount n. / number n.

It is not so much the meaning that causes confusion here, but the actual usage. Note: *He had a* **number of coins** *in his hand; He had a small* **amount of money** *in his hand.* And: *There were* **numbers of strong men** *in the park; There was a considerable* **amount of manpower** *in the park.*

The governing rule is this: When we speak of many individual units—"coins" or "laborers"—we use *number*. When we refer to a mass of a single nature—"money" or "manpower"—we say *amount*. Again: *a* **number** *of rifles,* but *an* **amount** *of firepower.* Note that *number* is used with a **plural noun,** while *amount* is paired with a **singular noun of collective sense.** Exactly the same rule pertains to the usage of *few* and *less.*

as conj. / *like* prep.

Remember the furor caused by the famous Winston cigarette advertisement: "Winston tastes good like a cigarette should"? For a brief time the correct form, ". . . as a cigarette should," was used. But then popular pressure won, and the incorrect use persists. What is the rule?

As is used as a subordinating conjunction introducing a dependent element and denoting comparison. In all cases where a verb follows or should follow, use *as*. Thus: *He speaks* **as I do**; *Do* **as I do**. Note also: He is **as tall as I** *(am); They are* **as happy as kings** *(are).*

Like is used as a preposition, and it must be followed by a noun or a pronoun in the objective case. *He looks* **like me**; *They sounded* **like men**.

The test is simple. If you can add a verb after the comparison, use *as;* if not, use *like.*

ascent n. / *assent* n., v.

Both words are pronounced alike ("uh-sènt"), but their meanings differ.

Ascent is a noun meaning the act of rising or going up. *They made the* **ascent** *of Everest.* A good device for remembering is to break it into two parts; *a scent =* scent is an odor = an odor rises = *ascent* = the act of rising.

Assent is either a noun, meaning approval, or a verb, meaning to approve or give approval.

avenge v. / *revenge* n., v.

Each of these words denotes a reprisal for injury. Usually *avenge* indicates the action of inflicting suitable punishment for injury to others. *One* **avenges** *the insult to a friend or neighbor*.

Revenge, on the other hand, implies a more malicious retaliation for injury done to oneself: *I'll* **revenge myself** *doubly for their humiliating me. Revenge* as a noun means the act of vengeance. *He took his* **revenge** *upon them*. It is also worth noting that *avenge* is almost always followed by a noun, its object. *I'll* **avenge** *the crime against me*.

athlete n.

Troublesome in only one respect: this is a two-syllable word, pronounced "àth-leet."

bail n., v. / *bale* n., v.

To be released from jail, one pays *bail* (n.) or someone else *bails* you out. In addition, one *bails* water out of a leaking boat. Cotton, after having been picked, is stored in *bales*. To put it into that form is to *bale* it.

bare adj., v. / *bear* v. / *bear* n.

Something which stands exposed or uncovered is *bare;* to expose something, or to reveal it fully, is *to bare* it. The verb *bare* has the following principal parts: *bare; bared* (past); *have, has, had bared*.

To carry something, or to withstand pain or unpleasantness, is *to bear* it. *Grin and* **bear** *it!* The principal parts of this verb are: *bear; bore* (past); *have, has, had borne*.

The great hairy creature, brown, black or white, is called a *bear*.

Note that all three words are pronounced the same way: "bare."

bazaar n. / *bizarre* adj.

Bazaar is a noun meaning a market place.

Bizarre is an adjective which means exotic, out of the ordinary, strange.

been v.

This is the past participle of the verb *to be*. **It is always used with another verb** (a helping verb). *I have been. He has been. They've been.* In American usage it is pronounced "bin."

being v.

Being is the present participle of the verb *to be*. As such it may introduce a participial phrase: **Being** *a good man, he pays his taxes cheerfully*. Sometimes it is used as a noun: *Man is a sensible* **being.** *Being* **is never used to introduce a dependent clause: Being he was hungry,** *he ate*. Even worse, **Being that** *he was hungry, he ate*. These two expressions, *being he* and *being that,* are simply incorrect. Instead, one says, **Since** *he was hungry,* or **Because** *he was hungry*.

berth n. / **birth** n.

A *berth* is a place in which one sleeps on a train or ship. It may also mean the dock at which a ship ties up.

Birth means the act of being born or created, as in *the* **birth** *of the blues*.

beside prep. / **besides** adv.

There is a fine distinction between these two words. *Beside* is a preposition. This means that it will regularly be followed by a noun, or by a pronoun in the objective case. *The spider sat down* **beside** *her. He walked* **beside** *me.*

Besides is an adverb which means "in addition to or also." Thus: *They brought bait to use* **besides** *what they would dig up.* Or, *He is a good leader* **besides**.

brake n., v. / **break** v., n.

A *brake* is a device which causes something else to slow down or stop, whether it is an automobile or a desire. *To brake* is to slow down and to stop. The principal parts of the verb *to brake* are: *brake; braked* (past); *have, has, had braked*.

The verb *to break,* meaning to smash or destroy, has the following principal parts: *break; broke* (past); *have, has, had broken.* Something which is broken is said to have a *break* in it. This *break* is, of course, the noun.

breathe v. / *breath* n.
The verb *to breathe,* pronounced "breethe," means to draw *breath,* pronounced "breth."

bridal adj. / *bridle* n., v.
Some cynical people might see a closer relationship between the terms than actually exists. *Bridal,* the adjective, means all things pertaining to a bride. *Bridle,* the noun, means the controlling headgear of a horse, and has been expanded to mean any form of restraint. The verb *to bridle* means to balk at something and to become annoyed.

bring v. / *take* v.
The meaning of each of these words is, naturally, well known to all, but the usage still causes difficulty. Remember it this way. *To take* means movement **away from the speaker.** *To bring* means movement **toward the speaker.**

burst v. / *bust* n.
Problems involving these words center on the encroachment of slang upon correct usage. *To burst* means to explode or to shatter suddenly. The principal parts of the verb are: *burst; burst* (past); *have, has, had burst.* The noun *burst* means the act of explosion or the rupture itself: *A* **burst** *of flame soared upward.*

The word *bust* is a noun for the part of a human body between the neck and waist, or a piece of statuary. To use *bust* as a verb, meaning to hit or to break, is slang and incorrect.

calendar n. / *calender* n.
The confusion here is based upon similarity of sound and the fact that the second word is not too well known. *Calendar* is the noun meaning a record of months and

days. Here is a good device for remembering the correct spelling: *calendar* = **days**.

Calender means a device for smoothing paper and cloth. As a verb, *to calender* means to smooth or press out.

callus n., v. / *callous* adj., v.
Here is a very interesting verbal problem. The word *callus,* a noun meaning hardened skin, has usually been regarded as a misspelling of *callous*. Actually, *callous* is an adjective (note the *-ous* ending) meaning hardened, coarse, or unfeeling. Both words may be used in verb form, meaning, respectively, "to form a callus," and "to make or become callous."

can v. / *may* v.
We all remember the time-honored tease of, *"Can* I go to the movies, Ma?" "Yes, you *can,* but you *may* not."

The distinction still exists in correct usage. *Can* means physically able to do something; *may* implies having permission to do something.

Calvary n. / *cavalry* n.
The problem here is sloppy pronunciation. *Calvary* is the place of the Crucifixion of Christ. It is pronounced "Càl-va ry."

Cavalry means horse soldiers, and it is pronounced as it is spelled: "càv-al-ry." There should be no confusion here.

capital adj., n. / *capitol* n.
Capital and *capitol* are among the most troublesome spelling words in our language. Let us conquer them.

Capital = adjective = main, principal, or chief. Remember the *a*'s." *Capital* as a noun refers to money or accumulated wealth. It also means a large letter in print or the principal city in a state or nation.

Capitol = noun = government building, frequently with a dome. Visualize the Capitol dome in Washington.

NOTE: *Capitol* with the *o* is used **only as a noun.** *Capi-*

tal spelled with *a* may be an adjective or a noun, depending upon its meaning and use.

censor v., n. / *censure* v., n.

When books are banned, and films cut, this frequently is the work of a *censor,* an individual empowered to delete, ban, or eliminate objectionable material. To perform this function is *to censor.* In each case the word is pronounced "sèn-sir."

The word *censure,* pronounced "sèn-sher," as a verb, means to rebuke or scold. As a noun it means the scolding or the rebuke itself.

chagrin v., n.

The difficulty with this word is only its pronunciation. As a noun or a verb, it is pronounced "shuh-grìn. It means vexation, humiliation, mortification, or the act of inflicting these feelings upon others.

champion n., v.

There is no such creature as a "champeen." He's a "champ-i-on," with all three syllables. If he's a winner, he should have them.

chassis n.

Chassis is a French word, naturalized into English but retaining its native flavor. It is pronounced "shà-see." Continued usage has permitted wider and wider acceptance of "chà-sis," but the first is the preferred form. It is interesting to note that almost all French words used in English retain their French pronunciation: *chef* = "sheff," *café* = "kafay," etc.

coarse adj. / *course* n.

Coarse is an adjective meaning rough or unrefined, and may be applied to salt, sugar or people. Visualize this: *coarse* = *adjective.* This word will usually appear modifying a noun.

Course is almost always used as a noun. Another good device for remembering is: *course* = *noun.* It means a route or direction or a routine state of things, as in *a course* of *study*.

column n. / *columnist* n.

One should encounter no problems with these words, but the addition of an invisible letter does make things difficult. The words are pronounced "col-um" and "col-um-nist." But there is no *y* in either word, either in sight or in sound.

competition n.

Spelling is the demon here. But if we remember the origin of the word, *compete*, we should be able to master it.

complacent adj. / *complaisant* adj.

Of these two words, the first is more familiar, but we do meet the second from time to time. *Complacent* is an adjective which means smug or self-satisfied.

Complaisant is also an adjective, meaning obliging, courteous or disposed to please. We can remember it, perhaps, by seeing its relationship to the French word *plaisir* (English *pleasure*): *complaisant* = *plaisir* = pleasing.

complement n., v. / *compliment* n., v.

Complement is a noun which means a crew or staff, or anything which completes something. The clue to the spelling is: *complement* = *complete*. As a verb, *complement* means to bring to completion.

Compliment as noun or verb means either praise or applause given, or to praise and applaud.

congratulate v.

Do we know the difference between the sound of "t" and "d;"? We do. Then we should have no trouble with "con-grat-u-late." There is no such word as *congradgulate*.

conscience n. / *conscious* adj.

The first word is a noun, pronounced "còn-shens," but it looks like *con-science,* and if we remember the *science* part of it, we will not be bothered by spelling difficulties.

Conscious is an adjective (note the *-ous*), and is pronounced "còn-shus." This is the simplest method of distinguishing one word from the other.

continual adj. / *continuous* adj.

Continual and *continuous* are both adjectives and very close in meaning. The distinction is a nice one, but it is important. Visualize a water faucet, not quite shut. The flowing water gets to the point of being a long, thin **unbroken line.** That is a *continuous* flow. Then it becomes an endless line of tiny, **separated, individual** drops. This is a *continual* flow. Thus, a *continuous* noise never stops; a *continual* din is occasionally broken by silence.

convert v. / *convert* n.

The difference between these words involves accent and part of speech. The first is a verb, meaning to change someone from one way of thinking to another, or to change something from one thing to another. It is pronounced "con-vèrt." The noun means one who has changed his thoughts or religion, and is pronounced "còn-vert."

corporeal adj. / *corporal* n., adj.

Corporeal is a **four-syllable word,** pronounced "cor-pò-ree-al." It is an adjective which means bodily, or having physical being.

The word *corporal,* a noun of three syllables ("còr-po-ral"), refers to a military noncommissioned rank subordinate to that of sergeant. *Corporal* also means bodily in *to suffer* **corporal** *punishment.*

consul n. / *council* n. / *counsel* n., v.

A *consul,* pronounced "còn-sul," is a diplomatic representative of one country in another land.

A *council,* pronounced "còwn-sil," is an advisory body, or a group of people acting to assist a ruler, governor or mayor.

Counsel, pronounced "còwn-sil," as a verb means to

advise, to suggest. As a noun, it means the actual advice given or suggestions made.

could of / should of / would of

These expressions represent the barbarian invasion of the precincts of language. They are the result of pronunciation and hearing. What is meant is *could have, should have* and *would have,* which in their contracted form become *could've, should've* and *would've.* But there are no such creatures as *could of, should of* and *would of.*

criticize v.

Spelling is the problem here. The way to remember the correct form is to see the word *critic* in the larger word: *critic-ize.*

curious adj. / curiosity n.

If we remember the pattern of endings which distinguish the various parts of speech, we can overcome the spelling difficulty here. *Curious,* the adjective, has one of the distinctive adjective endings *-ous.* The noun becomes *curiosity;* the *u* is omitted.

data n. / datum n.

Data is a **plural noun which takes the plural verb:** *The* **data are** *very clear.* The word *datum,* the singular form, is rarely used. In this connection we can see the tug between general usage and correct form. *Data* is used more and more widely with a singular verb: *The* **data is** *impressive.* But this usage is not yet **formally** accepted.

dearth n.

Here we have a simple matter of pronunciation. *Dearth* rhymes with *earth.*

debt n.

A silent letter makes an appearance here. The *b* is spelled but not pronounced: *debt* = "dett."

definite adj.

The slight trickiness in the spelling of *definite* can be overcome if we think, first, of the word **define,** and,

second, of the French *fini.* Put them all together, and
we have *definite*—just *e*'s and *i*'s.

deprecate v. / depreciate v.

The eye frequently plays tricks with words, and it is
easy to confuse *deprecate* with *depreciate.*

Deprecate means seek to avert by prayer, is now more
often used in the sense of to express disapproval of
something.

Depreciate is a verb which means to become less in
value; also to belittle or disparage. *His article was meant
to* **depreciate** *Darwin's book.*

desert' n. / désert n. / dessert n. / desert v.

Here is a pleasantly complicated little verbal family.
The distinctions among them become almost entirely
a matter of accent, spelling and knowledge.

The first noun (de-*zurt*) means worthiness of reward or
punishment, as in: *He got his just* **desert.**

Dès-ert" is a noun, and the only word of the group with
the **accent on the first syllable.** It means, of course,
a dry, arid, sandy waste.

"De-sèrt," accent on the second syllable, is a verb which
means to abandon, or to leave without permission: *He
refused to* **desert** *his post.*

The next, set apart by its spelling, is "des-sèrt," a noun
meaning the final portion of a meal, usually a sweet.
Here is a splendid technique for remembering: visualize
the double *s* as standing for "*s*weet *s*tuff." It may seem
childish, but you will never misspell or confuse the
word!

device n. / devise v.

Remember *advice* and *advise?* Here's another pair in
the same family. *Device* is a noun which means a tool
or an implement or a plan. Remember the final nouns
in the word itself, *vice* and *ice.*

Devise is the verb meaning to invent or contrive the tool, implement or plan; to make the *device*.

dive v.

Dive is a verb which causes concern only in the matter of its principal parts. Formally noted, these are: *dive; dived* (past); *have, has, had dived.* American colloquialism has spread the use of *dove* as the past tense. In choosing between that which is popularly acceptable and that which is regarded as correct, we should say *dived: The plane* **dived** *through the cloud.*

divide v.

The pronunciation is "di-vide" not "dee-vide," and therefore the spelling is *divide*.

draft n., adj. / **draught** n., adj.

These two words are identical in sound; but custom has reserved *draft* for a slight breeze and the calling up to military service. *Draught* is used for beer and nautical measurement, and, occasionally, in the plural, for checkers, or *draughts*.

drink v.

The past tense of this verb gives some trouble. The principal parts are: *drink, drank* (past); *have, has, had drunk*.

drown v.

There is no such expression as *drownded*. The principal parts of the verb are: *drown; drowned* (past); *have, has, had drowned.*

dye n., v.

Dye, noun or verb, means either a color to be added to a fabric, or to change the color of something. Retaining the *e* in spelling is important, especially in the present participle, which is *dyeing*.

elite n., adj.

Another French word taken into our language but retaining its foreign flavor is pronounced "ay-lèet." It is usually a noun, but may be used as a modifier: *elite corps, elite type.*

embarrass v.

Embarrass is troublesome only in terms of spelling. The very singularity of this word, however, makes it less of a problem: two *r*'s and two *s*'s make *embarrass.* This spelling holds true in all forms of the word: *embarrassing, embarrassment, embarrassed.*

emigrant n. / *immigrant* n.

The distinction between *emigrant* and *immigrant* is purely a matter of direction. An *emigrant* is one who leaves a country; an *immigrant* is a person who enters a country. Thus, you may *emigrate from* your homeland and *immigrate into* another country.

eminent adj. / *imminent* adj.

Eminent is an adjective meaning distinguished or important. The related noun is *eminence,* meaning a high position socially or politically, or a bit of high ground.

Imminent, also an adjective, refers to something which is about to happen.

envelop v. / *envelope* n.

Pronunciation and spelling set these words apart. The verb, meaning to enclose or surround, is pronounced "en-vèl-op." Note that there is no *e* at the end.

The noun, meaning an enclosure or container usually for letters, is pronounced "èn-ve-lope," and it does retain the final *e.*

environment n.

A very neat and effective device for remembering the correct spelling of *environment* emphasizes the word *iron* within it: *environment.* This is foolproof.

epigram n. / *epitaph* n. / *epithet* n.

Here are three frequently confused nouns. *Epigram* means a witty, pungent saying, usually summing up an ample thought in few words. *Whatever is, is right; I think, therefore I am.*

Epitaph is the name given statements usually inscribed on tombstones.

Epithet is a noun giving some peculiar or distinctive characteristic of a person or thing, such as Richard **the Lionhearted,** Alexander **the Great,** Elaine **the Fair.**

epitome n.

Before you go any further, jot down the number of syllables in this word. **Four!** "e-pìt-o-me." The noun means the very embodiment or essence of something, or an all-inclusive summary: *Helen was the* **epitome** *of feminine beauty*.

equipment n.

We have difficulty here because we do not let well enough alone. The word is *equip*. Add *-ment* and we have *equipment*. There is no *t* in the middle of it.

exaggerate v.

Once again the sequence of letters can prove confusing. Try to remember that the end of the word is the word *rate,* even though it is not written as one syllable: "ex-àg-ger-**ate**."

exalt v. / exult v.

A high mountain has great **alt**itude or elevation; to ex**alt** is to raise or elevate.

Exult is a verb meaning to rejoice or be triumphantly happy.

To remember the difference, bear in mind the *alt* = height.

exquisite adj.

Because this is such a delicate and precise word, it is only just that we accord it its proper pronunciation, the accent on the first syllable: "èx-qui-site."

extraordinary adj.

The surest way to remember how to spell this word is to think of it as two words: *extra* and *ordinary*. In pronunciation, it's only one: "extra**or**dinary."

faint v., adj. / *feint* v., n.

To faint is a verb meaning to lose consciousness, to collapse. As a noun it means the loss of consciousness or a collapse.

To feint is a verb which means to make a false or misleading move in order to throw someone off guard. A *feint* is the noun, meaning the deception itself.

fair, n., adj. / *fare* n., v.

The noun *fair* means a place where many products are displayed and sold, usually in an air of festivity. The adjective *fair* means pleasant, or just, or not particularly exciting, or light in color.

As a noun *fare* means money paid for transportation; as a verb it refers to the outcome of an action: *How did he* **fare?**

familiar adj.

Spelling this familiar word sometimes is troublesome. Let us think of it in relation to the word *family;* the *y* is changed to *i* and *-ar* added. Visualize the word *liar.*

farther adj. / *further* adv.

The distinction which used to exist between these two words is no longer insisted upon except in the most precise and formal usage. *Farther,* the comparative degree of the adjective *far (far-farther-farthest)* applies particularly to spatial distances: *Chicago is* **farther** *from New York than Boston. Further,* most frequently used as an adverb, applies principally to intellectual or intangible distance: *He could follow the complicated explanation no* **further.** In ordinary usage, however, these terms are now interchangeable.

ferment v. / *foment* v.

The basic difference between *ferment* and *foment* is that the former usually leads to excitement or delight, while the latter brings trouble.

To ferment, a verb, means to undergo chemical change, e.g., from grape juice to wine, or from hops to beer.

It can also mean, in drier terms, to seethe emotionally or intellectually, or to be agitated.

The verb *to foment* means to stir up unrest and discord.

fine n., adj.

The noun *fine* is well-known; it means a forfeit paid for violating a law.

As an adjective, it means elegant, superior, or delicate, thinly drawn, precise. Thus: *An architect draws a* **fine** *line on his blueprints; A* **fine** *wine.*

finger n.

A word of warning is necessary here. This word demands pronunciation of the hard *g*, as though it were spelled *fing-ger*.

founder n. / *founder* v.

This is the noun for one who establishes a foundation or who creates any institution: *He is the* **founder** *of the enterprise.*

As a verb, *founder* means to sink, or to stumble badly and fall. Neither word has any meaning-relationship to the verb *to find*.

fourth adj. / *forth* adv.

Here are simple words which cause trouble. The number is *four* and the adjective derived from it retains the entire word in spelling; **fourth**.

The adverb *forth* means forward in space or time.

friend n.

How strange that this, of all words, should prove such an enemy to spellers. But there's a sure ally. Remember this: friend to the **end** = *friend*.

fulfill v. / *fulfil* v.

These verbs, actually two faces of the same word, are annoying rather than really difficult. The first spelling, *fulfill,* is preferred. Remember it simply by counting one-two: one *l* then two *l*'s—*fulfill*. Or simply use the second form: *fulfil*.

gondola n.
Pronunciation is the problem again, rather than meaning or spelling. The accent is on the first syllable—"gòn-do-la"—whether we think of a Venetian boat or a railroad car.

government n.
Bear in mind that the noun retains the entire word *govern* and adds the suffix *-ment;* therefore, *government*.

grievous adj.
Let us test ourselves again. How many syllables in this word? **Two!** It is pronounced "grèev-us." Remember, two syllables!

hang v.
The verb *hang* presents an interesting psychological study. Perhaps it is because man is the only animal which kills and abuses its own kind for purposes other than eating. The verb *hang* has two sets of principal parts:

For objects: *hang; hung* (past); *have, has, had hung*.
For human beings: *hang; hanged* (past); *have, has, had hanged*.

To remember the correct past tense, bear this in mind: *hanged = man*.

hear v. / *here* adv.
The confusion between these two words is easily resolved if we see the relationship between *hear*, the verb, and *ear*.

The adverb *here* is the opposite of *there*, and defines one place in reference to another.

heard v. / *herd* n., v.
The kinship of *ear* and *heard* will enable us to make the distinction between the verbal past tense *heard* and the noun *herd*, which means a flock or group. The verb *herd* means to tend or drive.

hers pron.

 Hers is a possessive pronoun, one of the group characterized by not using the apostrophe: *yours, ours, theirs.*

hoarse adj. / *horse* n.

 Once again we may rely on the part of speech to help us remember spelling. The word *hoarse,* meaning harsh or gruff, is an adjective: *hoarse* = adjective. The noun is *horse: horse* = noun.

idle adj. / *idol* n.

 Again spelling and part of speech unite to help us. *Idol,* meaning an image which is worshiped, is a noun: *idol* = noun.

 Idle, meaning unoccupied or lazy, is an adjective.

impetus n. / *impetuous* adj.

 "Im-pe-tus," with three syllables, is a noun meaning force or energy, or, occasionally, stimulus.

 "Im-pèt-u-ous," four syllables, is an adjective (note the *-ous*) meaning rash or hasty.

impotent adj.

 "Im-po-tent," an adjective meaning powerless or weak, is pronounced with the accent on the first syllable, as though spelled, im-*puhtent.* To recall the correct pronunciation, think of the first part as *imp.*

ingenious adj. / *ingenuous* adj.

 Note the difference in spelling here. *Ingenious,* an adjective, means clever or inventive. Think of the sound and general meaning of *genius!*

 Ingenuous, also an adjective, means very innocent and gullible. Someone who bought the Brooklyn Bridge would be *ingenuous;* the salesman might very well be *ingenious.*

know v.

 The principal parts of the verb *to know* are: *know; knew* (past); *have, has, had known.*

 Remember that the negative is simply *no.*

laboratory n.

Frequently, in pronouncing this word, we slur the second syllable. The word has five syllables: "làb-o-ra-to-ry." The best way to remember both spelling and pronunciation is to think of *labor*.

lead v., n. / *lead* n. / *led* v.

The difficulty here involves a combination of physical resemblance—*lead* and *lead*—and similar pronunciation—*lead* (n.) and *led*.

To lead, the verb, is pronounced "leed." Its principal parts are: *lead; led* (past); *have, has, had led*.

We encounter the spelling *led* only in the past and past participial tenses of the verb *lead*.

When we use the word *lead* as a noun, meaning the position at the head of a column or in a race, we pronounce it "leed." But the word *lead* as a noun, meaning the metal (the element) or the core of a pencil, is pronounced "led."

leave v. / *let* v.

Here common usage has again encroached upon precise meanings. *to leave* is a verb which means to go from, depart or remove one's self from a person or place: **Leave** *the room!*

Let is a verb meaning to give permission or to allow: **Let** *him play.* Thus, when we say, **Leave** *him alone,* we are saying that everyone else should go away. What we actually mean is **Let** *him alone,* which means simply, "Don't annoy him!"

lie v. / *lie* v. / *lay* v.

These are three of the most troublesome verbs in the language. *Lie* is a verb meaning to recline, to stretch out. This verb is frequently followed by the adverb *down,* as in *to lie down.* Its principal parts are: *lie; lay* (past); *have, has, had lain.* Note the strange irregularity of form.

Lie is also a verb which means to tell an untruth. Its parts are *lie; lied* (past); *have, has, had lied*. Observe the regularity of form here.

The verb *to lay* is equivalent in meaning to the verbs *to put, to place, to set*. **It always takes an object;** that is, something **always** receives the action of this verb. Its principal parts are: *lay; laid* (past); *have, has, had laid*.

Remember: If you can substitute *put, place* or *set*, the verb should be *lay*. It is **always** followed by a noun or a pronoun: **Lay** *that* **pistol** *down, Babe!; Now I* lay me *down to sleep*.

like prep.

Like used incorrectly as a conjunction has already been discussed under *as*. But when it is a preposition we want, followed by a noun or pronoun, it's *like*.

loose adj. / *lose* v. / *loss* n.

The adjective *loose* is pronounced with a sharp final *s*: "loos." The verb *to lose* sounds as though (NOTE: not "like"!) it were spelled *looz*. And the noun is *loss*, again with a sharp *s* as in *boss*.

mad adj.

To be *mad* is literally to be out of one's mind, to be insane. What we usually mean when we use the colloquial form is that we are *angry*.

marital adj. / *martial* adj.

There might be an interesting psychological reason for one's confusing these two terms. Let us, however, say simply that they look alike.

Marital is an adjective meaning anything related to marriage. It is a three-syllable word: "màr-i-tal."

Martial, a two-syllable adjective, means warlike or military. It is related to the war god Mars, and we can remember the spelling that way.

medicine n.

> The confusion here stems from what follows the *med*. Just remember *medic,* and go on from there: *medicine, medical*.

mischievous adj.

> How many syllables? **Three.** "Mîs-chie-vous" is a familiar adjective and frequently mispronounced. **There is no such word as** "mis-chèe-vi-ous"!

moral adj. / *morale* n.

> The adjective *moral,* meaning just, ethical and good, is pronounced "mòr-al." The noun *morale,* meaning mental state or zeal, is pronounced "mo-ràl" and accented on the second syllable.

museum n.

> Another much-abused word is this noun. *Museum* has three syllables. It is pronounced "myu-zèe-um."

naval adj. / *navel* n.

> *Naval* is an adjective meaning anything that pertains to the navy. Remember it as *naval* = adjective, or perhaps *naval* = *battleship*.

> *Navel* is a noun meaning what is commonly referred to as a "belly button." It may be a little too strong, but *navel* = *belly* will help to prevent you from confusing or misspelling the word.

necessary adj.

> The confusion in *necessary* arises from the question, Two *c*'s or two *s*'s? Remember it as incorporating the word *cess,* or the simple count of one-two: one *c,* two *s*'s: *necessary*.

nice adj.

> *Nice* is another of the much-abused adjectives. It actually means very fine or meticulous. We vitiate its force and meaning when it is used to describe anything from "a nice time" to "a nice person." It should involve a *nice* distinction between two points or ideas.

ninety n., adj. / *ninth* n., adj.

Note that the word *ninety* retains the original word *nine*. The word *ninth,* used as noun or adjective, drops the *e*.

obligate v. / *oblige* v.

To obligate is a verb which means to put moral pressure on someone, to create a feeling that a favor must be returned. *To oblige* means either to compel, to force or, occasionally, to please. Sometimes there is a nice distinction between these meanings.

occasion n.

Here is another puzzler involving repetition of letters. Remember the gambling odds of 2:1, two *c*'s and one *s*. It is always thus: *occasion; occasional; occasionally.*

often adv.

While occasionally the middle *t* is pronounced, the most widely accepted pronunciation of *often* is "òff-en."

one n., adj. / *won* v.

If we keep in mind that *won* is the past tense of the verb *to win,* we should be able to avoid confusing it with the number *one.*

opinion n.

Careless usage causes trouble with *opinion.* Never say, "In my opinion, I think . . ." "In my opinion" means "I think," so you must choose one or the other: "In my opinion" or "I think."

ours pron.

Ours is another possessive pronoun distinguished by its lack of an apostrophe: *yours, hers, theirs.*

pain n., v. / *pane* n.

The two words are not related at all, but if you remember the word *paint,* you can use it to remember *pain.* If a wound *pains* you, you may **pain**t it with iodine or mercurochrome. By a process of elimination, that leaves us with *pane,* a noun meaning a window or a sheet of glass.

parallel adj., n., v.

Parallel provides its own aid in spelling. It takes at least two lines to be *parallel;* therefore we have two *l*'s before the one *l*. Visualize the lines first, then the *l*'s.

passed v. / *past* n., adj.

The verb is *to pass*. Its principal parts are: *pass; passed* (past); *has, have, had passed*. Therefore: *He* **passed** *the ball; They* **passed** *the house.*

But the noun or adjective which refers to times and places gone by is spelled with a *t*. Think of it this way: *past = time.*

peace n. / *piece* n.

If we can master either of this pair of troublesome words, the other will present no problem. The simplest way to defeat these twin terrors is to think of this: *piece,* the noun meaning a portion of or a share of, tells us— *a* **piece** *of* **pie.**

Then, since the other word has nothing to do with pie or portions, we can recall it as *peace,* or the noun which means quiet, serenity and lack of strife or warfare.

personal adj. / *personnel* n.

Here again our standard procedure clears the way for us. *Personal* is an adjective (note the typical *-al* ending) and is met as a modifier. Remember it as "pèr-son-al" = adjective, meaning anything pertaining directly to the individual.

Personnel is a noun, pronounced "per-son-nèl," which means the staff or crew of a group or institution.

picture n., v. / *pitcher* n.

In this instance spelling and pronunciation go hand and hand. The noun *pitcher,* meaning a jug or one who throws a ball, is distinguished by having the "itch" sound, formed with tongue and teeth.

Picture, used as noun or verb, is pronounced as though spelled with a *k* in the middle. When you say it, you should feel a slight click in the back of your throat:

"pìk-cher." With the proper sounds in mind, the correct spelling follows easily.

practicable adj. / *practical* adj.

The clue to the correct choice between these two terms lies in the word *able*. Let us see:

Practicable is an adjective of four syllables—"pràc-ti-ca-ble"—meaning capable of being accomplished or done, feasible. If something is *practicable,* we are *able* to do it.

Practical, also an adjective, means useful, a good idea, or it may mean the opposite of theoretical. Thus it may be a practical idea to build a bridge across the Atlantic Ocean, but it is hardly a practicable feat.

pray v. / *prey* v., n.

To pray is a verb which means to ask or beg for assistance or forgiveness, most frequently from a deity.

To prey is a verb meaning to hunt down and eat or destroy something. *Prey* is also the noun which means that which is destroyed or eaten. We can remember this distinction by remembering *to prey = eat.*

principal adj., n. / *principle* n.

Here are two more words high on the list of trouble-makers. Let us proceed systematically.

Principle is always a noun; it means ethical standard or matter of belief: *It is a matter of principle for a pacifist to refuse to fight.* Clue: *principle = ethic = belief* (noun).

Principal would be the spelling of every other use of the word. As an adjective—*principal = adjective*—it means main, most important chief: *The principal parts of the verb are . . .*" As a noun, *principal* means the head of an elementary or secondary school: *The principal is your pal!* It may also mean the chief sum in a bank account, as in *principal* and interest. Occasionally the word *principal* means the chief person in a transaction, as in *principals only.*

privilege n.

Privilege is a noun meaning special right or prerogative. We can overcome the spelling difficulty, if we recall that there is no *d* in the word—no *ledge* or *edge,* just *privilege.*

probable adj.

Again careless pronunciation is the enemy, and the word *able* is the ally. Recall that the word is "pròb-a-ble," the last part being the word *able.* In all the variations this same clue helps: *probably; probability.*

pronounce v. / *pronunciation* n.

Here are two words with which we are now quite familiar, and yet they are words which often confuse us, chiefly in spelling. The verb *to pronounce,* meaning to say or to utter, is pronounced "pro-nòwnse." Note the helpful contradiction; the **verb** contains the word **noun:** *pronounce.* The noun *pronunciation* may be remembered because it contains the word *nun: pronunciation.* And, of course, there is considerable difference between the sourds of the words.

prophecy n. / *prophesy* v.

Prophecy, the noun meaning the statement of what is to come, is pronounced as though spelled "pràh-fe-see." The verb *prophesy,* meaning to predict the future and state what you think will occur, is pronounced "prah-fe-sìgh."

psychology n. / *philosophy* n.

There is really no reason why these two words should give difficulty, but that, as we have seen, is no guarantee against verbal trouble. Once more, pronunciation is the key.

Psychology, a noun meaning the study of the mind, is pronounced "sigh-kòll-oh-gee." Note that the *p* is silent and that *ps* is always pronounced like an *s.* It may help to remember that the term stems from the name of Psyche, a beautiful Greek nymph. A more contemporary reminder is supplied by Alfred Hitchcock's moving picture, "Psycho."

Philosophy, also a noun, is pronounced "fill-àh-so-fee." It means the love of or study of knowledge and wisdom, and systematic organizations of thought.

q

NOTE: The letter *q,* whenever it occurs in an English word, is **invariably** followed by a *u.*

quarter n., v., adj.
Whether it be milk or soda, if you remember *quart,* you will remember the correct spelling of **quart*er*.**

quiet adj., n. / *quit* v. / *quite* adv.
Quiet may be used as an adjective, as in *the* **quiet** *man.* As a noun, it can be used this way: *He enjoyed the* **quiet,** or as a verb: *to* **quiet** *the mob.* The word has two syllables—*qui-et*—and is pronounced "kwiè-et."

The verb *to quit,* meaning to leave a place or to stop an activity, has only one syllable and is pronounced "kwit," to rhyme with *it.*

Quite, an adverb, has the silent final *e* which changes the sound of the *i* from the short "it" to the long "ite." Note also that the word has one syllable.

rain v., n. / *reign* v., n. / *rein* v., n.
There is not much to cling to in distinguishing these three words one from the other. Their pronunciation is the same, but their spelling and meanings differ.

Rain, a noun or verb, refers to the moisture dropped from the heavens and Lerner and Loewe's rhyme will help you remember it:

> The **rain** in **Spain**
> Stays **mainly** in the **plain.**

Reign, pronounced "rane," and used as a verb or noun, means either to rule or the rule or government, usually of a monarch. Remember the silent *g.*

Rein, a noun or verb meaning the strap which controls a horse, or simply to control something or someone, is also pronounced "rane."

raise v. / *raze* v. / *rise* v.

Usage rather than spelling confuses us here. The verb *to raise* **always takes an object.** You *raise* your *hand;* one *raises* the *roof;* they *raise* a *flag;* an organization *raises* funds. The verb means to lift (something) or to collect. The noun *raise* is usually used to mean an increase in pay.

To rise is a verb which means to get up, or to grow or to stand up. **It does not take an object.** Thus: You *rise* in the morning; the sun *rises;* the tide *rises;* dough *rises.* Note that nothing **receives** the action.

The verb *to raze,* which is related only in sound, means to destroy completely or tear down.

real adj. / *really* adv.

Here is a matter of abuse of perfectly good words. We frequently hear of someone who was **real** *glad* about something, or **real** *angry.* What is meant is *really.* Why? *Real* is an adjective and must modify a noun or a pronoun, as in *a* **real** *man,* or *a* **real** *value. Really* is an adverb, and may modify an adjective, verb or adverb: *He was* **really** *angry.*

A simple, foolproof test is to substitute one of the words *certain, certainly,* or *very.* Would you say, *I'm* **certain** *glad to see you?* No, you'd say, *I'm* **certainly** (*very*) *glad.*

The equation is: *certain = real; certainly* (*very*) *= really.*

recognize v.

If you remember to pronounce the *g*—"rèc-og-nize"— the spelling is simple. The spelling clue is the word *cog* in *recognize.*

recommend v.

Think of the word *commend,* to praise or to call to someone's attention. Then you simply re*commend,* and the *m* remains doubled, the *c* single.

rhyme v., n. / *rhythm* n.

With these two words, the very strangeness of appearance assists us. Just recall the unique and rather awkward sight of *rhythm,* pronounced "rĭth-m." It is alone among words. *Rhyme* starts the same way, but lacks the additional *th*.

ridiculous adj.

Correct pronunciation can help us here. Think of the word *rid*. It is ri**d**iculous, not r**ee**diculous.

rob v. / *steal* v.

When you *rob* a person, you *steal* something from him. Thus, the verb *to rob* means to take something **from a person or place** without permission. You **rob a person or place.**

To steal means to carry away or to take by force or furtively. You *steal* **something from** a person or place.

Thus, "to *rob* a bank," means to take money from it. "To *steal* a bank" would mean to carry away the entire building.

role n. / *roll,* v., n.

Role is a noun which means a part or a character one plays in a performance or a function one performs. *Roll,* when used as a noun, is a scroll or a small bread. As a verb, *to roll* means to sway back and forth, or to turn over and over, or to wrap or swathe.

rout v., n. / *route* v., n.

Here appearance should aid us considerably. *Rout,* as a verb or noun, is pronounced as though it were spelled *rowt*. It means a shattering defeat of a team or army. As a verb it means to inflict an overwhelming defeat.

Route, a noun meaning a road, a direction or a line of travel, is pronounced as though spelled *root*. It is a French word, and we have retained the foreign pronunciation. A team, then, is *routed* ("rowted"), but we sail a southern *route* ("root").

separate v., adj.

The verb *to separate* means to set apart or divide. And this provides us with a clue to correct spelling. Think of *par* and there will be no confusion in *separate*. As a verb, it is pronounced "sèp-a-rate"; as an adjective, we pronounce it "sèp-rit."

set v. / *sit* v.

To set usually means to place or put, and generally takes an object: Set *your* bags *down.* Equivalent to the verb *to lay,* it is governed by the same rules.

To sit means to occupy a seat. It is a verb which does not take an object. In attempting to determine which verb to use, remember this: If you can substitute *place, put* or *lay,* the verb is *set;* if you cannot, it is *sit.*

similar adj.

Frequently confusing in spelling, this is really a simple word. Pronounce it as it looks: "sìm-i-lar."

siren n.

There is no such word as *sireen*. Whether we mean the shrieking device on a police car or fire truck, or a lovely maiden who lures sailors to destruction, we pronounce it "sìe-rin."

stationary adj. / *stationery* n.

Two more heavy hitters in the problem league are *stationary* and *stationery*. First note that *stationary* is an adjective. It means not in motion or standing motionless. Recall the equation: *stationary* = *adjective* = *standing still.*

Stationery is a noun and refers to letter-writing equipment, principally paper. Here, then, is our clue: *stationery* = *paper.*

stay v.

To stay is a verb which means to remain or not to change. It may also mean to hinder or delay. Its principal parts are: *stay; stayed* (past); *have, has, had stayed.*

sure adj. / *surely* adv.

The situation of *sure* and *surely* is like that of *real* and *really*.

I'm **sure** *glad to see you!* Can you make the substitution: *I'm* **certain** *glad?* Hardly! We'd say, *I'm* **certainly** (*very*) *glad."*

Again the equation: *sure = real = certain; surely = really = certainly = very.*

surprise v.

A visual clue can help us here. If we remember the odd symmetry or *rpr,* we cannot misspell *surprise.*

teach v. / *learn* v.

You may *learn* something **from** someone, but you *teach* something **to** someone. Thus, the concept of *teach* usually involves **two objects, a fact taught to a person.** *Learn* involves only the idea of gaining knowledge of something.

tear n. / *tear* v.

As a noun *tear* is pronounced "teer." It means, of course, a droplet from the eye. The verb *to tear,* meaning to slash or rip, is pronounced "tare." Its principal parts are: *tear; tore* (past); *have, has, had torn.*

than conj. / *then* adv., n.

Because we do not really distinguish between these two in speech, they give us difficulty in spelling. *Than* is a conjunction, and it always conveys the meaning of a comparative relationship between two objects, one larger *than* another, or smoother *than* another.

Then, an adverb, always relates to a point in time. And that, perhaps, gives us a clue: *then = time.*

their pron. / *there* adv. / *they're* v.

This trio is probably the most frequently misspelled group of words in the language.

Their is a possessive pronoun. Notice that within the word itself is the word *heir,* meaning one who comes into possession of something. Our clue then is that when we want to use the word indicating ownership, it is *their*. Occasionally, we use the possessive form without the apostrophe: *theirs*.

The simple way to remember the spelling of the adverb *there,* used to point out location, direction or existence, is to see, within the term, its direct opposite, *here*. Again the clue is, *there*.

The last of the group should not cause any trouble if we remember its meaning. The contraction for *they are* is formed by dropping the *a* and substituting an apostrophe. *They're = they are*.

throw v. / *through* prep.

The principal parts of the verb *to throw* are: *throw; threw* (past); *have, has, had thrown*. The preposition, meaning penetrating or piercing, is spelled *through* and is pronounced "throo."

to prep. / *too* adv. / *two* n., adj.

To is a preposition indicating direction, and used in forming the infinitive or root form of all English verbs: *to see, to sit, to tell*. It has but one *o*.

Too is an adverb meaning in addition, as in *Take me* **too.** It also means to an extreme degree, as in *too expensive* or *too hot*. To remember it in this meaning, remember that it has an additional *o—too*.

Two is the noun or adjective meaning a number. If you keep its meaning and appearance in mind, you can easily remove it from the area of confusion.

victual n.

Every camper, hiker or viewer of cowboy pictures has heard the word "vittles." It means food. But its spelling is a matter of amazement: the word is actually spelled *victuals*.

weather n. / *whether* conj.

Weather is a noun, and it means the conditions of heat, cold, sun or rain prevailing out of doors.

Whether is a conjunction, usually used with the words *or not*, and indicating a relationship between two conditions or ideas.

who pron. / *whom* pron.

Who and *whom* are both pronouns. *Who* is the nominative case. We use *who* where *he, she, I, we, they* might be interchanged for it.

Whom is in the objective case. It would be used to stand for *him, her, me, us, them*.

Thus: (**who, whom**) *did you speak to? I did speak to* (**him, her, them**).

Therefore: **Whom** *should I speak to?*

whole adj. / *hole* n.

Whole, the adjective meaning entire or complete, is the longer of the two words. The noun *hole,* meaning a hollow or a gap, lacks the extra letter *w*.

woman n. / *women* n.

Carelessness can cause a little trouble here. **Wo**man is the feminine singular, just as *man* is the masculine singular. **Wo**men is the plural; *men* is the masculine plural. The plural form is pronounced as though it were spelled *wimmen*.

yours pron.

Yours is another of the possessive pronouns without the apostrophe, like *hers, ours, theirs, its*.

IX. SPELLING

"Ghoti."

Is it possible that you do not recognize this simple, familiar word? A common object! Something we mention or think about or see almost every day!

Obviously it is the word *fish*. Fish! How can that be? Let us see:

The *gh* is pronounced like the *gh in enou***gh**: *f*.

The *o* is pronounced like the *o* in **women**: *i*.

The *ti* is pronounced as though it were the *ti* in *nation*: *sh*.

Put them all together, and we have GHOTI = FISH!

George Bernard Shaw is alleged to have created this ridiculous spelling as part of his campaign to establish a phonetic system of spelling for English. Just recently, in England, a program has been launched among young schoolchildren to teach a new alphabet designed to facilitate correct spelling. Certain new letter combinations have been introduced in order to establish constant letter-sound relationships. Thus *ou* is to have the constant sound value of *ow* as in *flower*.

What all this indicates, of course, is that English is probably the most difficult language for a foreigner to learn. We have seen how perverse the grammar can sometimes be, how confusing the usage. And now we shall plunge into the morass of English spelling, an area of some rules, many exceptions and little consistency.

It is important to realize from the beginning that we do not have a system of phonetic spelling or pronunciation. What, precisely, does this mean? It means that we can not automatically determine, by the sound of a word, how it should be spelled, nor conclude from its spelling how it should be pronounced.

See the word *bow*. You cannot tell how to pronounce it. Do I mean *bow* to rhyme with *wow,* as in *bow-*wow? Or do I mean *bow* to be pronounced "boe" as in *He drew the* bow? We can judge only by the context of the sentence or paragraph.

Think for a moment of the clumsy combination *ough.* Look at its disguises:

*en*ough = uff
*b*ough = ow
*b*ough*t* = aw
*thr*ough = oo
*th*ough = oh

Pity the foreigner confronted with such dilemmas. And on occasion, pity the native, confronted with the many facets of his mother tongue.

What shall we do about it? Certain changes in spelling are being brought about through the great pressure of popular usage. We see *thru* and *slo* and *nite.* These spellings are not yet acceptable on academic levels, or in formal writing. They do make sense, of course, even though they may still look very strange. We do not, however, have any central academy, institution or foundation making a deliberate effort to establish a new system of spelling to be applied immediately and everywhere that American English is used. This, then, leaves a relatively simple approach; to overcome the difficulties which exist, we must learn to use correctly the forms at hand.

First we shall go through the alphabet and determine the various common pronunciations of which each letter is capable. This can bring us far along the road to spelling mastery, even if there is no perfect consistency in terms of sound and appearance. We shall establish two areas of pronunciation for each letter: primary, or most frequently encountered, sounds and secondary, or less usually found. As always, the beginning is the best place to start:

a	PRIMARY:	1. at, cap, hat = short *a*
		2. ate, cape, hate = long *a* or **name sound**
	SECONDARY:	1. affect, abuse = uh
		2. fatal, final = unaccented

b PRIMARY: An explosive lip sound which does not vary, as in but, abstract, crab.

| *c* | PRIMARY: | 1. city, facile, cent = s |

(To be pronounced like an *s*, the letter *c* **must be followed** by *i*, *e* or *y*.)

2. can, helicopter, cute = k

(To be pronounced like a *k*, the letter *c* must be followed by *t*, *a*, *o* or *u*.)

| | SECONDARY: | 1. cello = ch |
| | | 2. vicious = sh |

d PRIMARY: The *d* is a hard, unvarying sound formed by tongue and upper gum.

e	PRIMARY:	1. red, men = short *e*
		2. be, even = long *e* or **name sound**
	SECONDARY:	1. maker, faker = unaccented
		2. take, broke = silent

f PRIMARY: final, for, off = a sharp, pushed sound made with breath, lips and teeth.

SECONDARY: of = a *v* sound, made by lips and teeth

| *g* | PRIMARY: | 1. go, bag, grab = hard *g* |

(must be followed by a consonant or *a*, *e*, *i*, *o*, *u*)

2. age, gorgeous = soft *g* = dj

(must be followed by *e*)

| | SECONDARY: | 1. *gist, gibe* = dj (exception) |
| | | 2. *ing* = hard *g* (exception, as in *finger*) |

h   PRIMARY: h*otel,* h*elp,* h*urricane* = a heavy, blowing out between parted lips. The sound of letter *h* is not so much a sound as it is an outward breath.

     SECONDARY: *oh,* a*h* = silent

i   PRIMARY: 1. f*in,* s*in,* k*it* = short *i*
                 2. f*ine,* s*ine,* k*ite* = long *i* or **name sound**

j   PRIMARY: a hard sound formed by combining teeth, tongue and voice = dj, a pushed sound

k   PRIMARY: a clicking sound formed at the back of the throat, a hard *c*

l   PRIMARY: a sound formed by tongue behind upper teeth, plus voice

m   PRIMARY: a humming sound formed by placing lips together and using voice

n   PRIMARY: lips parted, teeth apart, tongue behind upper teeth, and voice

o   PRIMARY: 1. m*op,* l*op,* t*op* = short *o*
                 2. m*ope,* l*ope,* t*ope* = long *o* or **name sound**

     SECONDARY: w*o*men = i (exception)

p   PRIMARY: formed by popping breath through suddenly opened lips

q   PRIMARY: (NOTE: In spelling, *q* is **always** followed by *u*.) Pronounced like *k* usually with *w* sound immediately following: = kw.

r	PRIMARY:		a growling sound in the back of the throat
s	PRIMARY:	1.	*same, stamp, thrust* = sharp *s* = hiss
		2.	*mission, fission, tissue* = sh
	SECONDARY:		*is, was, his* = z
t	PRIMARY:		tongue behind upper gum, lips and teeth parted, sharp outward breath *hit, tub, brittle*
	SECONDARY:	1.	*nation, fraction* = sh
		2.	*capture* = ch
u	PRIMARY:	1.	*cut, run, dun* = short *u*
		2.	*cute, tune, dune* = long *u* or **name sound**
v	PRIMARY:		*violin, vane* = voiced sound
w	PRIMARY:		a shaping sound, a pushing of lips plus slight use of voice
x	PRIMARY:		*tax, mix, oxen* = ks
	SECONDARY:		*xylophone* = z
y	PRIMARY:		*you, yawn* = pushed-through sound
	SECONDARY:	1.	*silly, city* = ee
		2.	*myth* = short *i*
		3.	*thyme, rhyme* = long *i*
z	PRIMARY:		*zone, zero* = heavy, prolonged *s*

Improving your spelling, if not mastering it, becomes a matter of blending knowledge of letter sounds, knowledge of the visual appearance of words and knowledge of the few rules.

1. First among the last is the rule governing the order of *i-e* and *e-i*. Almost all of us recall the early schoolboy rhyme:

I before *e*
Except after *c;*
Or when sounded like *ay*
As in *neighbor* or *weigh.*

There are exceptions, of course, but the rule still represents a large, solid, reliable core. The chief variants from the rule are:

seize	*weird* (NOTE: *we-*ird)
either	*leisure* (NOTE: *lee-*sure)
neither	*financier*

2. Words ending with a *y* preceded by a consonant change the *y* to *i* before adding *-er, -ed, -er,* and *-est:*

try	*tri + es, i + ed = tries, tried*
boundary	*ari + es = boundaries*
happy	*pi + er; pi + est = happier, happiest*

3. Words ending with a *y* preceded by a vowel simply add *s* for change to plural or indication of tense:

say + *s = says*
day + *s = days*
donkey + *s = donkeys*

4. Words ending with a *y* preceded by a consonant change the *y* to *i* before adding *-ly, -ness, -ful:*

beauty	*beauti + ful = beautiful*
happy	*happi + ness = happiness*
fancy	*fanci + ful = fanciful*

5. In words ending with a silent *e* we retain the *e* when adding any syllable beginning with a consonant:

hope + ful = hopeful
life + less = lifeless
discourage + ment = discouragement
lone + ly = lonely

6. In words ending with a silent *e* we drop the *e* before syllables beginning with vowels, unless we want to retain a "soft *g*" (dj) or "soft *c*" (s) sound:

$$rope + ing = roping$$
$$believe + able = believable$$

but

$$courage + ous = courageous$$
$$singe + ing = singeing$$
$$notice + able = noticeable$$

NOTE: Sometimes *-ing* makes for an exception:

$$notice + ing = noticing$$
$$encourage + ing = encouraging$$
$$cringe + ing = cringing$$

7. In certain words, when we add *-ed, -er* or *-ing,* and want to retain the short vowel sound, we double the final consonant:

$$hop + ing = hopping$$

If we simply added the *-ing,* we would have the word *hoping* (hoaping).

NOTICE: $win + ing = winning$, or else we would have $wine + ing = wining$—more exciting, perhaps, but a different word.

8. In words of two syllables, ending with a consonant preceded by a vowel, when we add *-ed* and *-ing,* if the accent is on the second syllable, we double the final consonant:

$$refèr + ed = refèrred; \text{ but } rèference$$

Notice that it is *reference* because the accent is on the first syllable.

$$prefèr + ed = prefèrred; \text{ but } prèference$$

We sometimes find it difficult to form the plurals of nouns. Here again, certain rules do help:

9. Most plurals are made by adding *s* or *es* to the singular form:

$$dog + s = dogs$$
$$house + s = houses$$
$$box + es = boxes$$
$$fox + es = foxes$$

There is a natural logic about this spelling. It is possible and easy to pronounce the word *dog + s* as *dogs*. It would be almost impossible to say *box + s = boxs* without the additional syllable provided by the *es*. Hence the custom of adding *-es* to words which end with *s, z, x, sh* and *ch*.

10. Some plurals are formed by changes within the singular word. For this there is no set rule; only memory can serve here.

mouse	*mice*
man	*men*
child	*children*
loaf	*loaves*
tooth	*teeth*
woman	*women*

11. Certain compounded words have their plurals formed by changing only one part of the word:

brother-in-law	*brothers-in-law*
counsellor-at-law	*counsellors-at-law*
man-of-war	*men-of-war*

NOTE: When a word ends with *-ful*, its plural is formed by simply adding an *s*:

$$spoonful + s = spoonfuls$$
$$cupful + s = cupfuls$$

12. The possessive form of a word is made by using the apostrophe plus *s*:

$$boy + 's = boy's \ (hat)$$
$$horse + 's = horse's \ (hoof)$$
$$bus + 's = bus's \ (door)$$

13. If a long word ends with an *s*, we may form the possessive by adding just the apostrophe:

rhinoceros' horn
duchess' tiara

NOTE: These words are pronounced as though the additional *s* were present. Thus we say "duchesses tiara" though we spell only *duchess'*.

14. The plural possessive is occasionally troublesome unless we remember a simple procedure:

the word → its plural → apostrophe rule:
boy → boys → boys'
man → men → men's
child → children → children's

It is important to know that the item governed by the possessive rule is **the person or thing which does the possessing,** not the object or objects possessed.

In addition to indicating the possessive, the apostrophe is also used to denote a very special type of plural construction. For example: if we wish to state that the letter *s* appears in the word *possess* four times, we say, "There are four *s*'s in the word *possess*." We do the same with numbers: four 2's make 8.

The apostrophe is also used in contractions. It indicates that a letter has been omitted from a word. *They are* becomes *they're; it is* becomes *it's; they will* becomes *they'll.*

The following is an extensive list of words frequently used and frequently misspelled. Rather than concern ourselves, at this point, with rules pertaining to spelling, let us use one old reliable aid, the visual image. If you imprint certain of these pictures in your mind, of particular or unusual letter combinations, or of words within words, you will have little difficulty in remembering the spelling of the words involved.

absence	*already*	**bene**fi**t**	*city*
*absolu***te***ly*	*answer*	*bicycle*	*cities*
*ac***cept**	*argument*	*breakfast*	*clothes*
*ac***commo***date*	*attacked*	*calendar*	*cloths*
*acqua***in***tance*	*beauty*	*carriage*	*column*
address	*beautiful*	*carrying*	*committee*
alley	*beginning*	*ceiling*	*complement*
alleys	*belief*	*changing*	*compliment*
ally	*believe*	*choose*	*corps*
allies	*believable*	*chose*	*corpse*

couldn't	hope	peace	separate
council	hoping	peculiar	similar
country	hundred	picnic	sincere
countries	hungry	picnicking	sincerely
description	hurry	piece	stop
destroy	independence	plan	stopped
didn't	isn't	planned	successful
dinner	judgment	pleasant	successfully
disappear	knew	pneumonia	surprise
disappoint	lady	possession	surprising
disease	ladies	potatoes	taking
doesn't	lead	principal	theater
eight	led	principle	their
eighth	library	privilege	thought
English	license	pursue	thousand
envelope	loose	quiet	threw
extremely	lose	quit	through
familiar	medicine	quite	Thursday
field	minute	receive	too
fierce	mischief	receiving	try
fifth	mischievous	recommend	tried
foreign	museum	reign	true
forty	neighbor	relieve	truly
friend	ninety	relieving	twelfth
friendly	ninth	rout	weather
friendliness	occasion	route	Wednesday
government	occasionally	safely	whether
grammar	occur	safety	who's
handkerchief	occurred	Saturday	whose
having	occurrence	says	woman
height	paid	scene	women
hoarse	passed	scenery	writer
			written

X. VOCABULARY

At last it has happened! You've been caught in a TV nightmare. You're out in the middle of the desert at night, water's running low, and Old Paint hasn't much life in the old carcass. No Indians, thanks to the Seventh Cavalry, but you're lost! No trails, no signs, no highway markings. What to do? Where to turn?

You know that the nearest town lies due east. But how do you find east? Ah! The stars! You gaze up at a splendid spread of silver against the black. You spot a familiar constellation, the Great Bear, or the Big Dipper. You recall the old Army and Boy Scout routine. You find the two guide stars, measure off the prescribed distance, and there you have it, the North Star. With a whinny, a whoop and a holler you're off on the right angle, due east, toward town and a "Twilight Zone" awakening.

Now, then, let's come down from the stars to the work at hand, from constellations to vocabulary. Suppose you're lost with respect to a new word you've never encountered before. How can you start to figure out its meaning? Well, suppose you know what part of the word means! Let's go back to *constellation*. Let's pretend we don't know what it means.

We do remember, however, that *stella* is a word segment which has something to do with *star*. *Constellation*, then, must have something to do with stars. And *con* is part of a word meaning *together*. With some fumbling we can assemble a word meaning something pertaining to *stars* and *together*—which is, essentially what we mean by a *constellation*.

What we have demonstrated here is the use of **ety-**

mology, a study of the development of a word by analysis of its roots and origins. There are three parts of words that, when we know them, can help us determine the meanings of most words. They are called the **stem** (root), the **prefix** and the **suffix.** The root gives the word its basic meaning and usually appears in the body of the word. The prefix gives the word its direction. The suffix determines the use of the word, its part of speech.

As an example, let us examine the word *apathy*. You have never seen it before and can't figure out its meaning from the context. But a glimmer of light shines through. You recall that the word segment *path* has something to do with feeling or suffering or emotion, like **pathos**. And you are on the trail. The stem *path* does mean "pertaining to feeling or emotion," and it does derive from the ancient Greek word *pathos*.

It is true that this knowledge provides only minimal assistance, but it is a step forward. The prefix *a-* means *not* or *no;* and the suffix *y* indicates that the word is a noun, the name of some quality.

The word *apathy,* therefore, probably means "a quality of not feeling," or *indifference,* which is the correct definition.

What a clue this gives us for understanding other words! The prefix *sym-* means "for, together, toward"; and the prefix *anti-* means "against." Therefore, **sym**pathy is a feeling toward or for something or someone; and **anti***pathy* is a feeling against something, or a loathing or distaste for something or someone.

See how each section plays its part. The STEM is the core or heart of meaning; the PREFIX shows direction, for, against, with, without; and the SUFFIX indicates the nature of the word.

We present below a list of the most frequently encountered stems, prefixes and suffixes, which if properly used will stand us in good stead in our efforts to arrive at meanings of words and thereby to increase our ability to use more words more effectively.

ROOT	MEANING
ag, ig	act, urge, force
alt	high
aper	open, opening
aud	hear, hearing
cad (cas, cid)	fall
cant	sing
cap (capt, ceipt, cept)	take, seize, hold
carn (charn)	flesh
ced (cess, ceed)	go, yield
cinq (cinct)	enclose
corpos (corpor, corps)	body
cred	believe
cur (curat)	care
curr (cours, curs)	run
dict	speak
dign	worthy
dug (duct)	lead, bring
fa (fant, fat)	speak
fac (fact, fic)	make, do
fer	bear, carry
frang (fract, frag)	break
fund (fus)	melt, pour
ger (gerat, gest)	carry on, bear, bearing
grad (gress)	step, go
graph (gram)	write
jec (ject)	throw, hurl
junct (jug)	join
lect	gather, choose
leg	send
loc	place
log	word, science
loq (locut)	speak, talk
mir (mirat)	wonder
mis (mit, miss)	send
ped	foot
pend (pens)	hang, weigh, pay
pli (plicat, plex)	fold

ROOT	MEANING
pon (pos, posit)	place
spec (spect)	look
tang (tact, tain)	touch
vert	turn
vid (vis)	see
voc (vocat)	call

The prefix of a word gives us, in effect, its direction. We have seen that the stem *ject* means "to throw" or "to hurl." With various prefixes, we can "hurl" in different directions:

> *re*ject—to throw back
> *in*ject—to throw into
> *pro*ject—to throw forth
> *de*ject—to throw down
> *inter*ject—to throw between

Here is a list of common prefixes:

PREFIX	MEANING
a-	not, without
ab- (a-, abs-)	separation, away from
ad- (ac-, at-)	to, toward
ante-	before, in front
anti-	against
bene-	well, good
cata-	down
de-	down, away from
dia-	through
dis-	opposite of, apart, away
epi-	upon, for
ex-	out of, from
hyper-	excess
in- (in verbs)	into, toward
in- (adj. & n.)	not
ob- (op-, oc-)	opposition, against
pen-	almost
per-	through (time or space)

PREFIX	MEANING
pre-	before
sub-	under
syn- (syl-, sym-)	with, together
trans-	beyond, across
ultra-	beyond, extreme

The suffix is the terminating part of a word and serves rather like a keel, determining basically what part of speech the word will be. There are a few suffixes which become signposts to tell us immediately the nature of the words of which they are a part. Here are some common suffixes:

SUFFIX	MEANING
-able	capable of, able (usually adjective)
-acy	state of being, state (usu. noun)
-al	act of, relating to (usu. adjective)
-an	one who (usu. noun)
-ant	one who (usu. noun)
-ar	relating to (usu. adjective; sometimes noun); one who
-ee	one who, one to whom (usu. noun)
-eer	one who (usu. noun)
-er (-or)	one who (usu. noun)
-ful	full (usu. adjective)
-ian	one who is skilled in (usu. noun)
-ion (-tion, -sion)	state of being (usu. noun)
-ive	able to (usu. adjective)
-less	without, lacking (usu. adjective)
-ly	in such a manner (usu. adverb)
-ment	that which does (usu. noun)
-ous	fond of, characterized by (usu. adjective)
-tude	quality of (noun)

There are certain matters affecting the spelling of words which are related to the addition of prefixes and suffixes. For example, what happens to the word *satisfied* when we

add the prefix *dis-?* Is one *s* replaced by the other? Are
there two *s*'s? The answer is, fortunately, a very logical
one. If the word itself begins with an *s* the addition of a
prefix which ends with an *s* gives us a doubled letter:
dis + satisfied = dissatisfied.

If the word begins with a letter other than an *s* there
will not be a doubled letter: *dis + appointment = disap-
pointment.*

This same rule holds true, in principle, for some other
prefixes:

> *mis-*   *mis*spell
> *un-*   *un*necessary
> *im-*   *im*material

One suffix frequently added to words that remain other-
wise unchanged is *-ly.* The general rule is that this suffix
is simply attached: *lovely, immediately, attractively,* without any further changes. One important exception, however, is the word *true.* Here we drop the *e* to make the
word *truly.*

XI. LETTER WRITING

When Miles Standish sent handsome John Alden to woo the lovely Priscilla for him, he should have anticipated the "Why don't you speak for yourself, John?" And he also should have expected the final switch of grooms-to-be.

It is amazing, and somewhat dismaying, to observe that most of us, on most important, personal occasions, do send others to do our thanking, our congratulating, our sympathizing, and—horror of horrors—our wooing. It has become a big business to have people whom we don't know write the messages we send to our friends, wives, parents, beaux and ladies. And we are contented to accept the stereotyped, secondhand glory of being able to pick out a "clever card" or a "funny card" or a "cute card." Picking the card, not writing it, is supposed to make us "clever," "funny" and "cute," because it's such hard work to sit down and write a letter or a note or—and why not? a little verse for a lady on Valentine's Day.

Of course, it's easier to pick out the card. But what do we do when our clever card has won us audience with Lady Fair? Do we carry on conversation by flashing a succession of "store-boughten" cards which we have concealed in our sleeves? Remember Christian in *Cyrano de Bergerac?* Having gained a rendezvous with the fair Roxanne by using Cyrano's impassioned phrases, Christian finds himself alone and tongue-tied in the presence of his love, and he disgraces himself.

It is time, and long overdue, for us to assert ourselves as individuals and claim our own identity, particularly in personal, intimate matters. And surely a letter or little note or bit of verse **truly your own,** sent to a person close to you, will have a thousand times more meaning to the giver and the getter than the cleverest manufactured jingle on the market.

What are we asking? That everyone suddenly become a poet or a clever manipulator of words and phrases? Not at all. We are suggesting that, just as every individual gets to know his friends and neighbors and learns to live and talk with them **as himself** and not through a hired talker, so every individual can make friends with his own written words to reflect himself and his own thoughts.

During World War II many letters and cards went home bearing messages like this:

Dear Wife,
    This leaves me feeling fine. I hope you are the same.
                        Your loving husband . . .

This is simple and direct, and, certainly, for the soldier producing it with difficulty, personal. Some may be able to write more eloquently and elaborately; if we can, we should.

The problem is usually, "What can I say?" The answer is simple, "Just what you would **say.**" The letter should be yourself **talking on paper.** Are you well? Are you lonely? Are you happy? Did you meet a mutual acquaintance? Are you wondering about the children, the house, the dog? Let your letter be a chat. Don't worry about spelling, but don't fight it if you feel an urge to spell correctly!

If it's a matter of a greeting for a special occasion, think of something personal you know about the receiver of your note, some little quirk or whim which can be joked about good-naturedly by a friend.

The point of it all is that one must be one's own self and not try to hide behind another's words or gags. Don't we all feel a little chagrined when we read the names of the platoons of writers lined up to make a TV comedian seem to be funny? We admire a man who can frame and use his own materials and situations. While we are not all performers, we are all ourselves.

Perhaps the most important thing is to overcome our fears of our own feelings. We are usually reluctant to express ourselves, because we are afraid to sound "corny" or "silly." Any true and sincere emotion can be made to appear overdone and trite. But a true and sincere emotion, truly and sincerely expressed, manages to acquire its own stature and dignity. It's better to try to say what you feel, than to stumble around with "Aw shucks, 'twarn't nothin', ma'am."

The informal letter, while its content should be quite individual and personal, still follows certain forms in its appearance. Obviously, however, if you know a person very well, the form of the letter which you write is really quite immaterial. The usual form of the friendly, informal letter, is this:

April 28, 1962

Dear Frank,

_____

_____.

Your pal,
Roger

Just by way of contrast, a formal, business letter has this appearance:

2005 Pearson Street
Brooklyn 34, New York
April 27, 1962

Mr. John H. Smith
2017 West 94th Street
Hamilton, New York

Dear Sir:

_____

_____.

Sincerely yours,
Roger Goodman

XII. BOOK REPORTS

A dull book does not justify a dull book report. Whether you are reporting favorably or unfavorably, make your discussion sound as though you are interested in what you have to say. If there is a note of boredom or monotony in the report itself, the reader will never finish it. Why, if the reporter is bored, should the reader permit himself to be bored?

A good way to arouse interest is by starting with a question: "Have you thought of what it must be like to be absolutely alone on a lonely island in the middle of a lonely sea? When I read *Robinson Crusoe,* by Daniel Defoe, I discovered what such a life would be like."

Or perhaps start with a startling statement: "Two great, modern ocean liners, each equipped with the latest radar and radio equipment, one of them brand new and dubbed 'unsinkable,' sailing on courses which leave more than ample room for clearance, are doomed to collide, and one of them will plunge beneath the sea carrying fifty of her passengers. This may sound like a novelist's invention, but in reading *Collision Course,* by Alvin Moscow, I discovered how such a thing could actually occur."

Let the first paragraph of a written report contain the essential identifying information: title and author, and then the basic material of the work—what the story is about, or what subject the nonfiction work deals with, or something about the life of the person whose biography or autobiography you may have read. This should not be a painfully summarizing paragraph, but one which touches the highlights and points of greatest interest.

In approaching the second and third paragraphs of a report—this is really the heart of the task—you may go into some detail about a particular incident or character or idea which was of special importance to you. Here is where you mention specific happenings and quote the reactions of people in your story. While you illustrate what has gone on, your own point of view also becomes clear. Perhaps you feel there has been too much description; perhaps, not enough. Maybe the author has lost you completely in a maze of obtuse thought; perhaps he has become childishly simple. Whatever your own reaction —and it should be your very own—here is where you make it clear. At this point you may wish to mention something of the author's style of writing. Is there too much dialogue? Not enough? Are the characters unreal or dull? Are the situations removed from reality? Is the author too slick in dealing with important problems? The important point in all of this is that you must be putting your own personal opinions down. Do not try to recapture what you have read about a work, or what someone else has said. Whether you liked the book or not, let the opinion be your own.

In your conclusion tie all matters together with a final paragraph that sums up your entire reaction. Despite certain objections to the author's handling of material, or despite your feeling that there were definite misconceptions in the work, you may have found the reading challenging, provocative, worthwhile. All this should come out in your concluding paragraph, leading, perhaps, to a recommendation. If, on the other hand, your decision is negative, indicate your disapproval clearly. "For the reasons I have mentioned above, I cannot possibly understand how such a dull, confused, repetitious book could be made a best seller, or turned into a successful movie." Whether a reader agrees with your point of view or not, he should at least be able to identify it as yours.

Before actually writing a report, an outline should be prepared. This may be just a series of blocked paragraphs with sentences partly written out; or, perhaps, you may prefer a group of key words or ideas set down in sequence.

The rough draft follows. Though you should be reasonably careful at this stage, don't let your concern for style or grammar hobble your thoughts.

The final draft should be attempted only after you have gone over the rough draft with a fine-tooth comb, correcting every error you can find, strengthening and clarifying every thought. Above all, when revising your written work, do not fall in love with it. Rather, act as if you are perusing the work of your worst enemy; for each error you find, another pin is thrust into his waxen image. This is barbaric, of course, but it will help you improve your writing.

XIII. RESEARCH PAPERS

The research paper, or term paper, or term report, is something which remains with us from junior high school, through senior high, on into college—undergraduate and graduate.

A high interest level is, of course, essential. But even if the topic assigned is not particularly stimulating—"The Use of Elevators in New York Boarding Houses—1907–1914"—it becomes our duty to find some lively facet, some point of difference, some area of interest before we start our work. Obviously, the best first step is to pick a topic which is interesting and about which we know something. We can write best and talk best on what we know most about.

Sometimes, after selecting a stimulating topic, we may find that it is too vast to handle in one short research paper. Suppose we are interested in the topic of world peace. Can you imagine how many tomes, how many encyclopedias, how many libraries are filled with information and discussion of this area of thought? We have, perhaps, 1,500 words or 3,000 words in which to handle the problem. Our next step, then, is to limit our area of study. We may choose a narrower range of research: "High School Peace Movements of the 1930's—A Survey," or, "The Attempt to Limit Naval Armaments, 1918–1921." You may note that each of these "narrowed" topics is also potentially huge, but it is also possible to do a sound presentation in a carefully researched, well-planned term paper.

Having chosen a topic that you think you can handle, you are now ready to begin your research. Perhaps the first thing to do is to secure a pack of file cards—usually 3 x 5 cards are used—in preparation for your work.

The next thing, of course, is to find the necessary source material. First, check the entries listed under the subject heading in the library catalogue. Should you run into difficulty, never forget that school librarians and public librarians are always delighted to be able to assist a serious person who has a research task to fulfill. The librarian is frequently a neglected source of information and guidance.

Almanacs, yearbooks, encyclopedias and other standard reference works all will provide excellent leads for research. Do not, however, simply find the encyclopedia article which seems to fit the bill, and then copy it. This is cheating yourself more than anyone else. It is a waste of physical and mental power. It really accomplishes nothing. Use the encyclopedia article to get a broad view of your topic, and also as an excellent source of bibliography. For almost every extensive article in a reference work will have, at the end, a sound bibliography—a list of books and articles consulted in the preparation of the article you have just read. These are the primary, basic sources, to which you should turn in order to shape your own material and strengthen your own ideas. Depending upon the length and depth of your own research, you should probe deeply or skim through the other materials, picking out what you find interesting and necessary and choosing sections to quote from if you choose.

Use your 3 x 5 cards whenever you find useful material. A separate card should be used for each new item of information. The card should contain: (1) author's name, (2) book title, (3) page reference, (4) a key idea or quotation. Each card should be numbered in sequence.

When actually writing your report, you must make sure to give the proper credit to the original authors. There are two methods for giving this credit: the footnote and the bibliographical note. There is a form to be followed and certain symbols which are usually used:

1. **The Footnote:** When you have quoted a source or rephrased an idea derived from it, write a number, starting with 1 at the end of the section. Then, at the foot of

the page, repeat the number 1, and give the name of the author of the book, the title of the book and the page from which the material was taken:

1. John Smith, *The Other Man,* p. 349.

If your reference is a magazine article, the footnote is slightly different:

1. John Alden, "I Was the Other Man," *Redbook Magazine,* p. 37, November 11, 1959.

It frequently happens that we may have more than one reference from the same page of the same book by the same author. In order to avoid repeating the name of the book and the author, we resort to a Latin expression, *ibid.,* an abbreviation of the word *ibidem* which means "in the same place." The form is the following. First:

1. John Smith, *The Other Man,* p. 349.

Footnote number 2 is indicated thus:

2. *Ibid.,* p. 375.

And number 3:

3. *Ibid.,* p. 381.

Suppose, however, that there is another work which intervenes.

1. John Smith, *The Other Man,* p. 349.
2. Priscilla Alden, *Woman in the Case,* p. 11.
3. Smith, *op. cit.,* p. 356.
4. *Ibid.,* p. 381.

The *op. cit.* means "in the work cited," and makes it unnecessary to repeat the entire reference.

Actually, there are many ways in which footnotes may be prepared. Frequently high schools and colleges have their own preferred style, but what is briefly indicated here will serve as a starter.

2. **The Bibliography:** This is a list, in alphabetical order according to the author's name, of every work which you have referred to in preparation of your paper. If there

is no author mentioned, the item is placed alphabetically according to the first significant word of the title. The bibliographical item must make it possible for an interested reader to locate the book for himself. It should include:

1. Author's name—last name first
2. Title of the book—underlined
3. City of publication
4. Publishing firm
5. Year of publication

For a magazine article the basic form should be:

1. Author's name
2. Title of article—place this in quotation marks
3. Name of magazine—underlined
4. Volume and page number or numbers
5. Date

This is what a bibliography might look like:

Alden, John, "I Was the Captain's Messenger," *Redbook Magazine,* 12:37, November 11, 1959.

Alden, Priscilla, *Woman in the Case,* Boston, Houghton Mifflin Co., 1923.

Smith, John, *The Other Man,* Boston, Houghton Mifflin Co., 1918.

ANSWERS TO EXERCISES

Exercise 1B

spring, resumption, ritual, people, alarms, five, clock, morning, sleep, eyes, cars, drive, hour, hundreds, risers, roster, spot, links, hours, way, home, game time.

Exercise 2A

1. Frank told his father, Tom, that he ought to play golf.
2. Tom, Frank's father, explained to his son that he, Tom, could not play golf.
3. Tom's wife told her husband that he and his son should both play golf so that she could have some peace on Sundays.

Exercise 2B

1. They offered Mary and me a lift.
2. Mary and I refused.
3. Then he and Frank drove home.
4. Soon I noticed that Frank and he were annoyed.
5. So Mary and I joined Frank and him for a little drive.

Exercise 3

will be (s), should have, tend to be, stirs, is (s), would hit, count, point, is (s), settles.

Exercise 4B

1. The Joneses bought a (neat, attractive), new home.
2. They thought it was in a (trim, well-kept,) neighborhood.

3. They were thrilled by the (uninterrupted, broad) view of the water.
4. Then they noticed certain (disturbing, unfortunate) features of the house.
5. The (attractive, useful, functional) cellar kept the water in instead of out.

Exercise 5

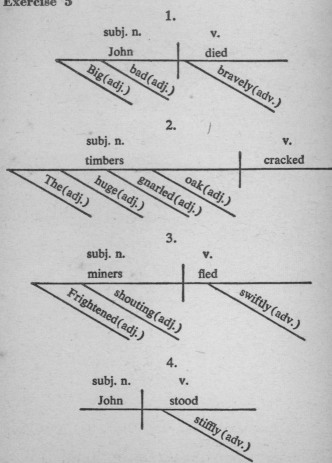

5.

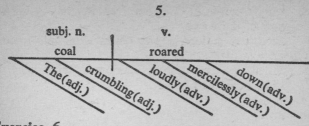

| subj. n. | v. |
| coal | roared |

The(adj.) crumbling(adj.) loudly(adv.) mercilessly(adv.) down(adv.)

Exercise 6

what!	interjection
is	verb
we	pronoun
read	verb
page	noun
of	preposition
technical	adjective
have	verb
is	verb
can learn	verb
this	pronoun
exercises	noun
little	adjective
tests	noun
really	adverb
part	noun
best	adjective
way	noun
to use	infinitive
tool	noun
it	pronoun
this	pronoun
of	preposition
grammar	noun

Exercise 7A

1. Subject: *sun*. Verb: *rose*. Object (of preposition *over*): *mountains*.
2. Subject: *you*. Verb: *Did see*. Object: *sunrise*.

3. Subject: *forest*. Verb: *threw*. Object: *shadow*. (Object of preposition *on: plain*.)
4. Subject: *It*. Verb: *was* (*beautiful* is a predicate adjective).
5. Subject: *You* (understood). Verb: *Look*.

Exercise 7B

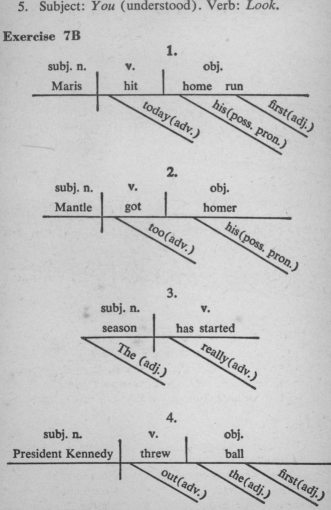

1.

subj. n.   v.   obj.

Maris | hit | home run

today(adv.)   his(poss. pron.)   first(adj.)

2.

subj. n.   v.   obj.

Mantle | got | homer

too(adv.)   his(poss. pron.)

3.

subj. n.   v.

season | has started

The (adj.)   really(adv.)

4.

subj. n.   v.   obj.

President Kennedy | threw | ball

out(adv.)   the(adj.)   first(adj.)

5.

subj. n.	v.	obj.
Mets	will win	pennant

The(adj.)   immediately(adv.)   their(poss. pron.)

Exercise 7C

1. They came out of the blue!
2. (Complete sentence.)
3. I have never seen a flying elephant!
4. Haven't you really seen one? It is like something out of Disney.
5. (Complete sentence.)

Exercise 8A

1. *that was produced abroad:* modifies *film.*
2. *who made it:* modifies *stars.*
3. *that everyone covets:* modifies *prize; which gleams in its case:* modifies *statuette.*
4. *who works behind the scenes:* modifies *man.*
5. *who patiently sits through the poorer films:* modifies *viewer.*

Exercise 8B

1. *When the moon shone bright:* modifies *crept.*
2. *while he approached:* modifies *grazed.*
3. *whenever he heard them whinnying:* modifies *froze.*
4. *If they smelled him:* modifies *would panic.*
5. *when a great stallion approached:* modifies *ran.*

Exercise 9A

Grammar . . . importance.	Simple
Not really.	SF
One . . . ungrammatically.	Complex
Jimmy . . . orate.	Compound
They . . . friends.	Simple

But . . . question.	Simple
Is . . . correctly?	Interrogative
Would . . . well?	Interrogative
Are . . . car?	Interrogative
Language . . . set.	Simple
If . . . other.	Complex

Exercise 9B

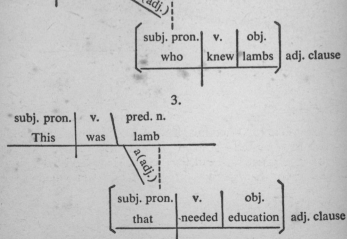

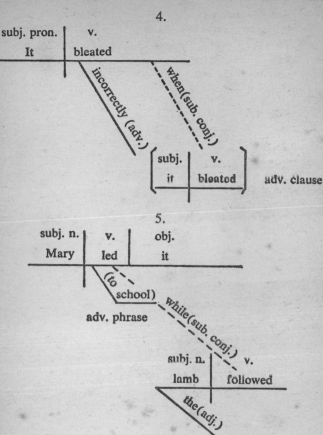

4.

| subj. pron. | v. |
| It | bleated |

incorrectly (adv.)

when (sub. conj.)

| subj. | v. |
| it | bleated |

adv. clause

5.

| subj. n. | v. | obj. |
| Mary | led | it |

(to school)

adv. phrase

while (sub. conj.)

| subj. n. | v. |
| lamb | followed |

the (adj.)

Exercise 10

1. journeyed—had imagined
2. had pleaded—granted
3. had argued—decided
4. gave—had given
5. released—had held
6. had—heard
7. have entered
8. has not ended

Exercise 11

1. are
2. was
3. was
4. is

5. are   8. are
6. has   9. represents
7. are   10. rules

Exercise 12A

1. Because he had his radio turned on full blast, he could not hear the fire siren.
2. Looking into the rearview mirror, he could see a huge, roaring hook-and-ladder truck.
3. With a shout of fear he swerved toward the sidewalk.
4. The driver wiped his brow as the firemen drove past yelling.
5. As he pulled away from the curb slowly, you could see that he had learned his lesson.

Exercise 12B

1. carefully   4. good—good
2. good   5. carefully—well
3. they

Exercise 13

When mankind passed through the grunt-and-groan stage, and language had been invented, everyone was happy.

"Communication has been established," they said, "and now we can understand each other."

Then writing was developed so that words could be given some durability.

"How wonderful!" everyone exclaimed. "Now we can read and write."

But then they began to have difficulty understanding what was written down, because everything seemed to run together.

"How confusing!" they complained.

So they invented sentences and phrases and clauses and punctuation.